MO
11.—

To my wife,

whose gentle perceptions

and understanding

encourage

the thoughts I share

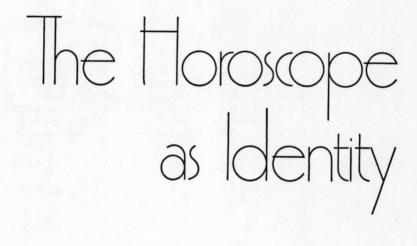

The Horoscope
as Identity

Noel Tyl

Llewellyn Publications
Saint Paul, Minnesota 55165

First Edition 1974

Llewellyn Publications
Post Office Box 3383
Saint Paul, Minnesota 55165

International Standard Book Number: 0-87542-799-5

Library of Congress Catalog Card Number: 73-20069

Printed in the United States of America

Preface

This book assumes that the reader can easily and accurately construct the horoscope for any given birth date, time, and place. It assumes the reading of aspects, a familiarity with classic meanings of relationships, rulerships, progressions, and transits.

My effort here is to give to the conceptions of awareness, ambition, and sexuality a modern treatment within a modern time. The considerations put forth are shared with the reader through many, many actual up-to-date examples. I share my observations not to compete in any way with the styles, deductions, or writings of any other astrologer. Rather, in awe of the lore that has become ours, I submit one man's service with it, within the time that is life itself. For the opportunity, I am deeply grateful.

Noel Tyl, summer, 1972

Contents

115   **Sex in Freer Times**

168   **Speed-Reading the Horoscope**

The Horoscope as Identity

1

What is the awareness we feel of others? What do we instinctively perceive when we meet another through car windows at a traffic light, rushing across a crowded intersection, catching someone's eye at a party, sensing our spouse's thought, mood, wish?

Every person seems to have some highly distinctive identity, communicated in some way, infinitely swiftly, to another's particular sensitivities. Some call it "aura", ESP, rapport, love, spirit, etc. How the communication is made is indeed a telepathic mystery. Is it ray emanation, electrical projection, animus transference, compassion, observational sensitivity and experience? Knowing *how* certainly would be a colossal glory to the development of intelligence and the entire field of consciousness. Knowing *what* is registered between identities, however, is possible now, definitely, and seeing *the horoscope* as identity within the frame of time, interaction, and fulfillment increases the rewards of Astrology. Astrology illuminates the identity, its position in the time of living, in the interaction with others, and in its evolution toward fulfillment.

Ancient writers depict man's dignity among animals by virtue of his erect posture, his upward "bend" toward the

1

heavens, raising his eyes to the stars. Indeed, the eye is a marvel: a tiny lens admitting the celestial immensity. Our observations give countless impressions to our being. We see that others see too—awareness—and it is our power and sensitivity of observation that regulate our level of identity awareness. We can see as far as natural conditions will allow (atmosphere, obstruction, curvature of the earth); our sensitivities (disciplined by knowledge, of course) help us see much "farther", help us to new levels of awareness, to the recognition, understanding, enjoyment, and shaping of the identities that are man.

The horoscope charts the heavens at a particular moment in a particular place. It is the immensity admitted through the newly born lens, finding focus in awareness and life. The natural conditions are recorded, and understanding them gives man vision, direction, and challenge.

The horoscope is what we are, what we are becoming. It is what we "communicate" to others. It is the composition of the aura, the "stuff" of ESP, the base of rapport, the attributes that condition love and loving. —The flash of recognition or intense interest with a stranger or loved one is theoretically something an astrologer can find in the horoscopes of the identities involved. The range of correspondences between the two can be from a fleeting sexual interest to a deep karmic recognition. In marriage and business relationships, of course, these interrelations observable through chart comparison are very important matters. But it is in the casual moment, the dissociated awareness—the pause in traffic, helping a stranger, enjoying a play for the same reason as that person over there, twelve rows away—that make us aware of the remarkable energies involved, the enormous communication power of the identity, the incredible importance, expressibility, and potential of the horoscope.

Old Astrology texts were written in slow times. Our century of speed, travel, expansion, and myriad opportunities absorbs future shock in an instant. Our identities play in a larger arena;

the scope of our horoscopes' potentials is extraordinarily enlarged. Where identity change and growth in the past centuries were checked by many variables including economy, disease, government, isolation, and society, **change** and growth are *expected* in modern times. In the past, people often were executed for being individualistic. Today, in Western culture, people *must* specialize; individuation is demanded. Travel opportunities enable people to go to "better conditions" for improving growth: the asthma patient can change his climate, the artist can seek cultural outlets especially suited to his personal statement, the businessman can relocate for better markets and personal advancement.

Such changes can be remarkable. "I haven't seen him for several years; my, he's changed!"—this popular remark is less a statement of surprise now than it used to be. Now, it is a recognition of all the dimensions operating upon individual and collective identities to do more, to be more. Weight-control courses can change the body; psychiatry can adjust the mind; religion can transform the spirit; a change of profession can free potentials. These resources are at our fingertips; such alterations are fad and fashion. In working with the modern pace of change, we are exploiting the potentials of our identity, our horoscope, more intensely—and sometimes more dangerously—than men have in all past time! The astrologer works to know this identity, to help its communication and development with maximum economy and security.

"He's changed"—his horoscope has "progressed." The progressed Sun shows the stage of self-development at the progressing time. The progressed planets show how different activities and identity values cooperate with the progressing life-force: Mercury, the mind and mental faculties, the attitude; Venus, the emotional reactions and aesthetic responses; Mars, initiative and impulse; Jupiter, the higher mind, the enthusiasm, scope of reward; Saturn, the architecture of advance, structural change; the Moon, concrete events and psychological needs.

Progressions are always built upon the birth chart, of course. Identity is communicated through their dynamic interrelationships. The aura, the feeling, the identity emanated by a person says so much so quickly about these interrelated factors. Horoscopes and progressions "communicate" with each other: the immensities recorded at different moments, born of the same celestial drama, recognize each other. Is this a meaning of "All men are created equal, " i.e., from the same source at a different moment? Is this the astrological aesthetic that helps us to understand and appreciate the many colors within humanity?

Every astrologer feels uncomfortable with the question of fate and free will. Certain transits and progressions seem to correspond to certain occurrences with a degree of predictability that, on the one hand, delights us for the evidence provided that Astrology really has "scientific" dimensions, and on the other, introduces an element of fate, of causal relationship, that diminishes the integrity of free will—the very ingredient of change that honors the gestalt of identity. Things are made easier when we allocate the progressed aspect and/or transit to a genre of "possibilities" and give free will the rein to establish the level. But it's all too easy to forget the total identity—the whole of the horoscope in its time of life—in the excitement of a concrete aspect or transit. We lose the integrity of the whole if we lose sight of and appreciation for the aesthetic coherence of the individual identity.

In the chapters that follow, we will see how Saturn can be more friend than foe, how sex in a broader, more modern understanding spreads its ego and creativity potentials *throughout* a horoscope, how periods of development have a modern timetable in an age of travel, specialization, and enormous demands for self-realization. More than ever before, we must adjust the identity's communication within the enlarged arena. For example: Pluto is only in its "early forties" as far as modern astrological analysis is concerned. The conjunction of

Saturn and Pluto in Leo, absorbed in the horoscopes of all born between the fall of 1946 and the end of 1948, immediately after World War II, means something unique to us. No astrologer ever considered it before! No astrologer ever saw a horoscope with this conjunction in it! No astrologer ever lived in the times we live in now. How do we interpret this conjunction in our modern time? The ancient legends that *are* Saturn, Kronos, time itself, buckle in relationship with Pluto, often interpreted as the herald of the twentieth century, the world-century, in the Sign which is the polar complement of Aquarius, the grand age at whose dawn we all now stand. The identities born under this conjunction need to defend themselves against the press of time and life: time (Saturn) and masses (Pluto) coalesce in cold ambition in the sign of authority, personal honor, glory, and life itself (Leo). The identities demand attention, recognition, accolade. Our modern time presents a broad spectrum from which to choose a cause, a goal, a means, a stage for this need for attention: internationalism offers politics (and revolution), incredible travel possibilities offer every man a choice of place in the world (and a hijacking opportunity), racial issues inspire humanitarianism (and sedition). Perhaps this conjunction *is* the much-touted "generation gap"!

Although astrologers weren't aware of it, and it was rarely in Leo, this conjunction did occur many times in the past (every thirty-two to thirty-four years or so; previously in 1914 and 1915, in Late Gemini, early Cancer). Then, however, fewer identities absorbed it (fewer were born), and society and the times presented fewer outlets for the thrust determined by conjunction Sign and House placement. The energies were more confined and, because there was no awareness of Pluto, perhaps Saturn was given the *whole* burden of manifestation, the signification of the *previous* generation gaps. We inherit the observations from then, but we must adjust our analyses to the present.

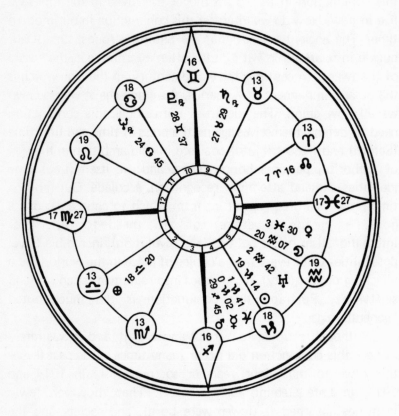

Modern times permit longer lives, great ascendancy, rises and falls, an enormous spectrum of level, and a challenge for fresh interpretation of eternal movements and aspects. Another example: when Saturn made its second return to its radix position in President Nixon's horoscope in the springs of 1971 and 1972 at 27 Taurus 29, retrograde in the IXth House (Nixon: 9 January 1913, 9:44 PM, PST, 118 West, 33 North), one knew there would be a change in the direction of his life. This always seems to happen when Saturn returns at ages twenty-eight to thirty and fifty-six to sixty. Surely, he would make a powerful decision to affect his entire way of progress, in IXth House affairs: foreign travel, philosophy. This anticipation was reinforced because of Saturn's elevation and rulership of the Sun's Sign Capricorn, occupying half of the IVth House (new beginnings) with Mars, Mercury, and Jupiter clustered there between 29 Sagittarius and 1 Capricorn; and because Saturn is squared by the radix Moon in Aquarius in the VIth House (work, service), trined by the Sun on the Vth cusp, and trine Uranus in its own Sign Aquarius. Nixon wasn't going on a foreign trip for a quiet vacation! He heads a country in the space-age. With a four-year contract, he could hardly "change jobs" or retire! He was bound to make an enormous foreign policy decision, affecting the masses (Pluto in the professional Xth), putting everything he was—his life energy, his personality, his work, his individuality, his energy, his mind, his judgment—into play. —He journeyed to China and then to Russia and made history.

Now, what about a man born at nearly the same time as Nixon, in the same year, in Southern California. He might be a taxicab driver, maybe a fleet owner by his 59th birthday. With this same vitally important transit, he too would have made quite a whole-hearted decision, involving his energies, individuality, judgment, wife, etc. *He* could easily have planned an early retirement, taken his first trip abroad, perhaps into the Pacific to

Hawaii! He would have had the same progressed New Moon the year before in 18 Pisces, near his seventh cusp. He would have seen a new way of meeting the public, and at 60, possible retirement and the beginning of a new period in life.

The difference here is simply the level of the identities, conditioned by parentage, society, education, friends, opportunity, and the expectations of modern times: the level of fulfillment of the Moon-square-Saturn thrust, the management of the Sun opposed Neptune, the Mercury-Mars-Jupiter opposition to Pluto in the Xth. His identity development would have had difficulties similar to the series of "crises" Nixon has written about. —The objective analysis of the horoscopes would not be able to separate public president from private businessman. But how *he* felt about *his* life as it progressed, in relation to the lives of those around him, would constantly lead him to *his* level, *his* comfort. The astrologer needs the client's own views as much as he needs the birth information, especially in modern times with few surprises and vast possibilities, when "anything goes." Nixon's views and progress are public. Every astrologer has him for a client!

The *scope* of response possible in these modern cases is a scope not known in earlier times, when lifetimes were halved, when travel was rare, when ambition was restricted.

Perhaps this is why horoscopes are so much easier to read *after the fact,* with historical perspective. How easy it is to suspect Martin Luther's sexual motives for church reform! How smart we are to "see" so clearly the Duke of Windsor's death! After the fact. Centuries remove the threat of correction; report of death puts us on the trail for confirmation. But Astrology is an act of *sharing.* We need an awareness of social times to appreciate the scope of opportunity. We need the client as much as he needs us. The level of communication between astrologer and client unlocks the nativity. To *prove* Astrology, we often seek—or are forced—to perform a miracle of divination. We have no sight of the identity in such a situation; we see only aspects and astrological recipes. Our vision can only be incomplete.

The core of an identity is the sought-after "key" to the horoscope. Sometimes, a client speaks it himself in his first sentences. Public figures give clues all the time. Sometimes, it is terribly difficult to find, usually when the astrologer looks through his own eyes—or is compelled to—and not enough through those of the client; or when he doesn't value highly enough *the call for specialization and acceleration typical of our times.*

This call is the press of the environment upon the identity. Nixon's crises, his "double's" tough times. The press creates anxiety as well as drive and ambition. It magnifies sadness from underachievement as well as glory from overachievement. The case studies included in this book will cover this press and discuss again many of the points put forth above, as well as relating individual identity to philosophical viewpoints and improving astrological service.

The core of identity is elusive. Discovering and articulating it is Astrology's art form and discipline. Astrologers spot the importance of clusters of emphasis in the horoscope. These clusters or stellia are welcome beginnings to finding the key. Pasteur's horoscope and Luther's are well known examples. We spot the absence of oppositions or squares as another hint, a lack of focus in the horoscope, in the identity's alinement within potentials. We sometimes find that the constellatory emphasis behind planetary clusters, key zones, or key planets themselves (usually including several "fixed" stars) offers a far-reaching wholeness with which the analysis can begin. Considerations of the New Moon preceding birth can suggest a karmic counterpoint within the present life. *Our eye takes in the immensity indeed,* but to begin with the nearest observation too easily shortens the focal length of our vision. Looking to the grandeur of the whole—the times, the opportunities, the social expectations—is to revere the miracle that is creation, respect the blessing that is life, and help understand the challenge that is formed in the horoscope, the horoscope that *is* identity.

2
Saturn in More Modern Times

Saturn is time itself. Saturn is the taskmaster of any horoscope, the staff-sergeant keeping the identity's forces in line. Saturn's reputation for melancholy, coldness, constriction, sorrow is overwhelming—perhaps too overwhelming!

Saturn was regarded as so evil an influence that, because it ruled the last day of the week, the people of the Bible established a day without work, a day to keep people at rest, out of trouble! The mortality rate in ancient times was almost twice what it is now. Sicknesses ran rampant, plagues developed unchecked, accidents were critical. Cause had to be found. Saturn's legend, distance, and slowness took the responsibility. As we will see in more detail later, Saturn's period corresponds to the development of social identity: starting school at six to seven (first square of Saturn to its radix position); adolescence at fourteen to sixteen (the opposition); out of college, able to vote at twenty-one (second square); professional change of way, maturity at twenty-eight to thirty. The cycle continues with corresponding stages to considerations of retirement near sixty (second revolution), and continues further, aided by welfare and social security benefits. In ancient times, life was compressed

11

into those *first* thirty years. Sickness and governmental strictures upon the individual wiped out identity early indeed. Astrology was in the hands of the priests and savants. Life was mystically linked with an anthropomorphic animation of the celestial movements. *Cause had to be found for the hard times in order to vindicate the religion.*

We inherit the poetic rules and interpretations of that early time. Sepharial, a scholar of antiquity, in all his excellence as an astrologer and thinker, succumbed to the ancient legacy of deified causal lore and predicted the end of the world, the "coming of the Prince of Peace by 1932 or 1936. . . . The earth will be strained to the breaking point. . . . this earthquake is destined to effect the beginning of the end." Saturn was to be square Mars-Jupiter and the opposing Neptune in late April, 1926.[1] The transit of Saturn over the eclipse line on 4 June 1928 was to bring "Armageddon."

Astrologers had a difficult time *establishing cause* for the Black Death of 1342, until the conjunction of Mars, Jupiter, and Saturn occurred three years *later.* We all know of the complicated and arbitrary applying-and-separating time schemes relating the superior planets' conjunctions and eclipses to mundane duration, providing explanation of events.

Alan Leo *does* submit that directions sometime fail because of a man's higher evolvement, an identity's higher level. *But, in more modern times, man is at a higher stage of evolvement, collectively and individually.* Society has so many more benefits, so much more time, so much more acceleration, and the individual has so many more opportunities and aids toward self-realization.

Mercury takes on infinitely more significance in relation to modern man. Internationalism often demands learning new languages, travels of hundreds of thousands of miles in a lifetime.

1. Queen Elizabeth II was born 21 April, 1926!

In older times, only the select could read and write, could enjoy travel. Today we have medicines and therapies for nervousness, the modern disease of an overactive Mercury.

Jupiter becomes dramatically significant in the light of modern education opportunities, higher learning, and the need to assimilate all the wisdom and science of past history and time.

Competition and the spirit of free-enterprise give many more acceptable outlets to the energies of Mars; sanctions for for freer sex give more outlets to Venus and Mars.

Modern times stress the exponent of individuality as the power to build and maintain progress. The Uranian individual is at a premium in a time of discovery, invention, and identity expression.

The art worlds and the dissemination of previously guarded occult mysteries give significance to Neptune, never known before 1846. (Alan Leo says that Neptune allows the soul to leave the body. Prior to Neptune's discovery, the sensitive soul was rarely acknowledged, let alone allowed to bring rewards to the identity through expression. What planet could have corresponded to Neptunian inspiration then? If we take Neptune out of Dante's horoscope, sacrificing the square from Uranus—unknown in Dante's time also!—the sextiles to Sun and Mercury and the Ascendant, we lose the indication of much of his identity's very own inferno and paradise.) The world community and revolutions of all kinds now demand recognition of Pluto.

Saturn was overworked in past centuries before the discovery of Uranus, Neptune, and Pluto. In modern times, Saturn "works" in more particular dimensions. Saturn is a "specialist" for specialists. Its leadership must marshall so many facets of identity with infinitely increased opportunities to express themselves. Perhaps this modern challenge is the "higher side" of Saturn so often referred to as "out of man's reach." Before the discovery of Uranus, Neptune, and Pluto, Saturn was the end of the line, figuratively and literally. We've inherited an uneasiness about Saturn, a legacy of bugaboos, that threaten to depress and constrict development in more modern times. Perhaps it is not Saturn that "causes" constricted development, gloomy interpretations. *Perhaps it is constricted analyses that don't allow anticipation of challenge, organization of forces, strategy of determined development.*

One established Astrology author even goes so far as to state that no one with Mars square Saturn in the birth chart can hope to achieve something enduring, something significant, lasting, memorable! How would you like to tell that to parents exultant at the birth of their child (to the parents of Charles Dickens, with Mars square Saturn), to a dynamic businessman approaching a big business deal (like J.P. Morgan, with Mars square Saturn), to someone fighting hard to regain health? Such powerful statements about Saturn, even about the square aspect generally between any bodies, distort our vision. A so-called difficult Saturn leaps out of the horoscope drawing even before we have all the positions recorded. Astrology books almost seem to fall open to those Saturn pages, those "squares," those evocations of capitalized "FATE" and promises of difficulties.

In "busy" horoscopes, we must synthesize many, many aspects. The dramatic ones seem to predominate, but perhaps the very multiplicity of aspects dilutes the singular ones. For example, we have the saying, "Jack of all trades, master of none." The multiplicity mitigates the singular. Or we have the saying, "I'm too busy to worry!" Preoccupation helps to overlook what to someone more idle is critical—simple distraction, the magician's misdirection.

The times and the environment change from century to century, from generation to generation, government to government. Savanarola was a religious revolutionary. He was executed because he was dissonant with his times and government, not "because" of his Mars-square-Saturn in the birth chart. In our modern day, he probably would be a world figure, enjoying our times' philosophic freedom. Mary Baker Eddy, founder of Christian Science, with Sun-square-Saturn, also might have been executed in Savanarola's Florence, or perhaps she might have escaped with her life, though sacrificing her identity, by living when women, by definition, had nothing to say.

But there is no doubt that for Savanarola and Mary Baker Eddy, Saturn was a powerful taskmaster. Each responded to Saturn's leadership: Savanarola through his fiery personality (Moon conjunct Mars) clash (square) with Church authority through personal ambition (Saturn); Mary Baker Eddy through her life-energy (Sun) giving new church structure (Saturn in the IVth) to the public (Sun in the VIIth). Each faced obstacles and criticism (squares). They persisted, and history (Saturn) records their work.

Saturn definitely can be linked to difficulties, to challenge, to demand upon the system. Each identity carries its own crosses. Without struggle, we have no growth. Think of the enormous effort for a new spring plant to break through the surface of the earth, hardened by winter and ice, lured by the challenge to reach the Sun. Think of the famous who have overcome debilities only to overachieve where many would have succumbed. *Saturn defines an architecture of advance.* Modern times change "architectural" needs and styles, expanding responsibilities and opportunities for identity expression.

Other horoscope factors modify Saturn's leadership. But maybe we can understand development more positively by seeing Saturn as calling the other constituents of the identity into action—the architect's using materials differently—rather than "causing" something and our identity's then running to the rescue.

For example, once we experience the progressed Moon's square to the birth and/or progressed Saturn (Saturn's slow movement and retrograde periods keep its radical and progressed positions relatively close throughout life, especially in relation to the swift Moon), we experience opposition, square, conjunction, and square again every seven-and-a-half years. Indeed, this is where we get the "seven year" sayings in our language, "the seven-year itch," "seven years bad luck."

At these times, things happen. We have ups and downs. To progress while walking, we literally fall and rise with each step. To develop while living, we constrict and enlarge our resources, our muscles contract and expand, sorrow alternates with joy. Change is simply impossible without tension. Noise defines silence.

Freudian influence in the twentieth century has taught us that we shun pain and seek pleasure in life. Contrast this with Eastern thought in which silent endurance and stoic patience absorb stress, in fact establish an entirely different concept of time for individual evolution. The registration of Saturn seems different at different times to different people in different philosophies. Certainly, the challenge to every individual in every time is unique, and so must be our analyses.

The "ups and downs" may be the pain en route to pleasure. The pain defines the pleasure. The cycle of Moon to Saturn by quadrants is *the call to action.* We gain expansion, development, growth from this tension, from constriction, if you will. The muscle contracted is stronger than the muscle relaxed. The tone of the muscle when it is flexed is the characteristic of Saturn in the birth chart, growing throughout the progress of identity fulfillment. Man seems to know this instinctively, yet he fears difficulty, challenge, responsibility to a surprising degree. His language embodies the fears of fate, the thoughts of a good God, the hope for development, and the expectancy of effort in the adage, "Everything happens for the best!"

In *Astrology for the Millions,* Grant Lewi brilliantly defines the transit of Saturn through the horoscope. He delineates dramatically what seems to happen to the identity as Saturn transits the four quadrants, its own position, and the other bodies. The architect makes his rounds.

Lewi describes the identity as in "relative obscurity" while Saturn goes from the Ascendant to the cusp of the IVth House; the "new beginning" as the IVth cusp is touched; the re-emergence into the public eye as Saturn ascends to the Midheaven; the gradual fading of achievement as Saturn descends once more to the Ascendant. —The architect prepares plans, begins to build, shows progress to the public, completes the structure, enjoys the achievement while fading in importance, and then begins to plan anew.

Lewi's studies dramatize meaningfully the horoscope's angles and the planets positioned throughout the chart. Depending on Saturn's starting point, an identity can enjoy two or three full-bloom periods in life. With Saturn near the Ascendant at birth, full ambition recognition (Saturn transiting the Midheaven) will be possible around twenty-one and fifty-one years. Saturn at the Midheaven at birth brings the high points around thirty and sixty years. At the same time, for the first identity, a very powerful shift in life would be expected upon Saturn's return to its birth position near the Ascendant at twenty-eight. For the second identity, a dramatic change of ways would occur as Saturn comes to its own place near thirty, a period of regrouping forces from thirty-six to thirty-seven until forty-two to forty-five, then a new beginning and climb. Of course, the angles will measure varying numbers of years due to varying latitudes and resulting Sign interceptions, prolonging or shortening quadrant periods.

The dynamism of Saturn's rounds is built upon its transit relationship to its own position, then to the Sun itself (life energy), then to the angles of the horoscope. At the same time, the progressed Moon's position in relation to the radical and progressed Saturn delineates the development of the personality's

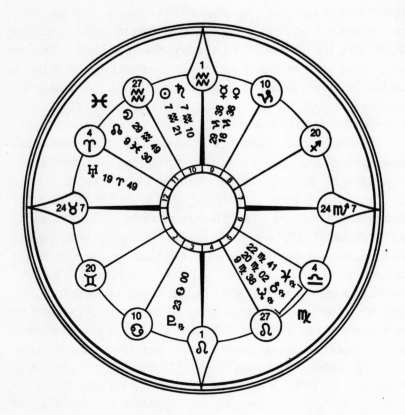

form within the environmental changes. —It is uncanny how these dimensions get into phase with one another, how, instead of a maze of measurements, a consolidation of considerations emerges, providing an architecture of advance to the identity.

The horoscope on page 18 is a clear example. The native has Saturn conjunct the Sun at the Midheaven in Aquarius without major aspect. This is quite a fusion of life energy and ambition—soaring flood-lit ego. The fixed Signs on all angles, which hold Sun, Moon, and Saturn, would give a tenacity to this ego. The highly elevated Mercury is extremely important as ruler of the Vth House cluster in Virgo. These three: Neptune, Mars, Jupiter (and the South Node) are all retrograde and intercepted. Uranus rules Aquarius (with Saturn), is limited by the XIIth House position, and is squared by Venus, ruler of the Ascendant

The native is a powerful people-person. The Aquarian emphasis with the Moon in the XIth certainly tells us he needs people in one way or another: to serve them, to have their help, to gain their recognition. In every sense, he's a public performer. The trine between Mercury and Mars-Jupiter is excellent, invigorating and expanding mental abilities. The retrogradation and interception factors here, in the House of creativity and art, would help us anticipate shifts in energy output, mental attitude, philosophy during the life.

The native was a foreign language teacher, became an opera singer, and now plans another major shift of identity development.

Venus rules the Ascendant as well as the VIth House of work and sickness. Posited in the IXth in Saturn's Sign, we get a further corroboration of educational outlets, an indication of a foreign "aesthetic" and work in foreign countries. The square to Uranus in the XIIth would help us wonder about individuality limitations *in relation to* the creative energy and a shift of thinking suggested by the Vth House. This square in Cardinal

Signs also would suggest sudden nervous expenditures and the breaking of social restraints.

The native journeyed to Europe to pursue an opera career, after having taught a foreign language in public schools; he felt confined wherever he was: devising unique yet unappreciated teaching methods, performing well without the rewards he expected. He is a Jew and sensitive to religious discussion and tension, especially in Germany. (Interestingly, his Ascendant degree is the Sun's degree of the State of Israel.) Under pressure, he develops a nervous tic (socially embarrassing to him) in his neck (Taurus Ascendant-ruler Venus, lord of the VIth, square Uranus in the XIIth, parallel Mercury, Mars parallel Uranus).

These elements of the identity can be seen quickly and corroborated with the native by a few questions and minimum discussion. But where is the identity going; what plan can the various dimensions follow; what is the architecture of advance? Let's follow Saturn.

We know that Saturn would be at its peak of recognition as it approached and passed the Midheaven, dramatically so, since Saturn would return to its birth position, make the conjunction with the Sun, after having touched Venus and Mercury and what we have seen they represent. This would have occurred between twenty-eight and thirty years. Saturn came to the Midheaven (with Mars) and then made the conjunction with its radical position in February through March of 1962. The native surely was rewarded for his ambition and ego professionally (Xth House), involving a build-up of foreign and aesthetic hopes; a reward to facilitate a new direction for the identity.

In 1961, with Saturn conjunct Mercury in the IXth, the native was awarded a Fulbright scholarship to study music abroad. In February through March of 1962, he prepared for an international music contest in a foreign country and won a significant prize two months later in May, when the progressed Moon opposed the radical Jupiter in the Vth (opposition is the "awareness" aspect), trined the radical Pluto in the IIIrd (communications, public), and sextiled the Ascendant. His life had changed. The ego was at its brightest.

The native came to this astrologer in the fall of 1969, seven-and-a-half years later. He had been given a fine contract at an important opera house in Germany. The identity was in full blaze, and Saturn was nearing the Ascendant. Grant Lewi points out that Saturn, as it approaches the Ascendant and retirement into the northeast quadrant, establishes a peak, a kind of bow before the curtain at the end of performance. The beacon in the radix Midheaven was beaming powerfully for the native, but another shift was yet to come. Another mighty bloom could be expected near sixty years. What was the architect going to plan in the meantime?

The native was helped to understand that in the spring of 1971, Saturn would cross the Ascendant (and that of his wife's horoscope a little bit later), that a reorganization was possible in order to do more in the years ahead. The suggestion was respected but discarded, until the press of the environment early in 1971 brought pressure upon the identity.

Here were the difficulties of Saturn. Here was the "downfall" described in all the older books. Going full-throttle into this period would be a debilitating shock indeed—ignoring the call to wisdom that *is* this transit. But positively, in this modern time, with travel and educational opportunities abounding, studying the deepest personal needs and redirecting energies would relieve frustration and perhaps bring the final shift in identity development to enjoy bloom near sixty.

The Pluto position in the IIIrd House in opposition to the elevated Mercury stresses the native's extraordinary communication ability, projected to the masses internationally; his keen awareness of "resurrected" Judaism and the land of his fathers; his wanting desperately to find a home for his talent, for his identity. The "higher octave" of Saturn—perhaps the level of

Saturn to which *modern man can* now tune—is definitely ministerial. Here in Aquarius, these high levels of humane service through the talents of the identity can beckon. In discussion with the native, Saturn's call came to disclose a private dream: to become a cantor and serve the call of his people's religion with the creativity of his music and intellect.

The native lost his nervous tic almost completely as he talked about this potential. Suddenly, *Saturn's call was no longer onerous.* Travel and study—financed through careful budgeting and sacrifice (Saturn)—would provide a new emergence in people-service as Saturn climbed again toward the VIIth cusp and then returned to the Sun.

Let us look again at Saturn's orbit in relation to its radix position to see its etching upon the emergence of an individual into modern society. For sake of abbreviation, let us give Saturn the symbolic meaning of ambition. In Caesar's time, men were slain for ambition. In modern times, not to be ambitious is to be bypassed by progress. Ambition is the means of expansion. Its power frightens man's instincts: he knows ambition will separate him from his group, upset momentary social security in order to make changes, shift levels or standards. Ambition is man's prerogative, his free will. In his position within time, ambition is his developmental duty. Management of ambition is his art of living.

Ambition grows in the child through the model established by the parents (particularly the father, Saturn). The parents project it upon him, and he absorbs it as independence. At six to seven years, Saturn squares its birth position: ambition potential registers as the first steps toward independence. The child is put out of the home to go to school. The timing of this process seems almost universal. Modern educators say the child is ready to learn much earlier, that learning is a continuous process. But, as yet, time and experience have ordered society to beginning formally the child's education at this first Saturn-square-Saturn transit.

Seven years later, Saturn opposes its birth position: ambition stares itself in the face! *The opposition is an awareness aspect.* The young organism of fourteen to sixteen years sees its identity potential clearly for the first time. The glands work overtime. The identity responds to recognition. In earlier times, young men in adolescence were leading armies. Their life span urged them *to be* at an earlier age. Their societies needed and used them earlier than modern societies do. There is much more to learn in our times. Society keeps the young ambition at rest, delays recognition and practical application of the talents until more learning is acquired, until seven years later at twenty-one, when the identity becomes an adult, graduates from college, is able to vote, drink, marry without parental consent. *The adolescent crisis is a frustration of identity awareness.*

At twenty-one, the closing square of Saturn's own orbit, the identity takes its first position in society; ambition, its first steps, its first job. The identity flexes many of its dimensions; many mistakes are made, hasty marriages, wrong jobs. The young identity is out alone, but still it is on uncharted ground: Saturn has not yet been through one round of the horoscope. Feeling free, the identity makes many stabs at fulfillment, dreams are fired, jobs are changed, resources are managed recklessly. The House stress in the Horoscope, the dimensions of the identity come into play without complete design, without a full blueprint, without mature perspective.

As Saturn nears its birth position, ambition seems to sense a coming focus. Preparation begins two to one-and-one-half years before Saturn's return, and the free will is brought into action, maturity is aroused, ambition is anchored. Here, the identity makes a choice that usually determines the route of its next seven years, or fifteen, or thirty, until near retirement. Suddenly, there's a generation gap with others who are younger!

At thirty-five to thirty-seven, we experience the first square again—another time of potential shift. Remembering the first square at six to seven, we can expect an echo. Saturn has been over the ground once already. Perhaps the business firm ("home"-office) gives the identity further recognition, further independence, grooming him for still further development. By this time in the life, other planetary periods are developing, some more quickly; decisions are mounting up, identity is crystallizing. There are more variables at work, but all hang upon Saturn's frame, his architecture.

Second adolescence indeed is possible between forty-two to forty-five. We feel we have something more to say, more ambition to show. We expand, spend, look for fresh challenge, throw security to the winds, and feel a "second youth."

By sixty, society and time plan for our retirement (but not in Eastern societies). Lewi reports that no president of the United States (from Lincoln to Franklin D. Roosevelt, inclusive) who experienced Saturn's second return while in office was ever reelected or, if reelected, survived the term. There was only one exception, Woodrow Wilson, who had Saturn in the ninth House while the country was in a foreign war. But he left the presidency totally discredited.

There is a second one now: President Nixon, also with Saturn in the ninth House while the country is in an international war. Will he be reelected? Will he regret deeply having been reelected?[2]

Society belongs to time and change. Saturn's orbit certainly parallels the emergence of identity through society's structure. Just as the writings of astrologers give us a picture of the mental attitudes of their times, so does Astrology itself—the timing of divine purpose—create a blueprint for mankind, picturing some mystery of mysteries.

2. This book was written in 1972.

In the example under discussion, the orbit of Saturn in reference to its birth position closely follows its orbit in reference to the angles, and of course to the Sun's position. The analysis is optimally clear.

In the example on page 26, positive life development in modern times clashes with old-style expectancy of failure. Only Saturn is above the horizon, retrograde at the Midheaven. Saturn is the handle of the "bucket," to use M.E. Jones's description of this planetary configuration. In a very real sense, the identity "swings" from this Saturn handle. The identity is lifted, tilted, poured out, and filled by Saturn. The powerful bundle of Mars, Uranus, Venus, Jupiter, Mercury, and Sun, all within fifty-one degrees within the Ist and IInd Houses would immediately suggest a powerful personality (Ist), oriented to money (IInd), and energetic (Mars), individualistic (Uranus) self-projection of an expanded (Jupiter) aesthetic (Venus-Jupiter, Jupiter-Mercury), which would bring considerable profit (Sun in Taurus in the IInd). The Moon (the personality's form) in conjunction with Pluto in Cancer would suggest grand creativity (Vth), emotionally oriented (Cancer), going to the masses (dexter conjunction with Pluto). Neptune is stationary in the VIth, trined by Jupiter and Mercury (Jupiter ruling the Xth, the profession, and the Pisces Ascendant, with Neptune): the employment is not quite what it seems to be (Neptune in the VIth); the native's enthusiasm (Jupiter in Aries) and his mind (Jupiter and Mercury) work well with the intangible, and maybe are "somewhere else."

The native, an American, was director of a world-famous international advertising firm, stationed in Germany. His experience, expertise, and salary were enormous. Ambition obviously had paid off. When he came to this astrologer, he was six months before his forty-fourth birthday. Immediately, one could know that Saturn was approaching the second opposition to its birth position, the second "adolescence." The opposition

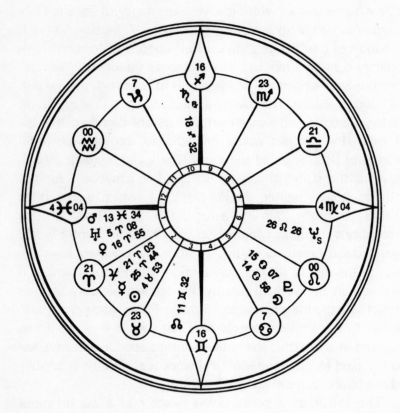

to come would occur at the fourth cusp: a new beginning? What of the past seven years or so when Saturn would have traversed the northeast quadrant? Was the native, in his obvious professional and financial "glory," really "relatively obscure"? Adding forty-three to forty-four degrees (his age) to the Sun's position, progressing it approximately, would bring the Sun to an opposition with radical Saturn, moving just past conjunction with the fourth cusp! Saturn in retrograde motion would surely still be on the Midheaven through progression. This was a dynamic moment in life indeed!

The IVth House is certainly well known as the "end of the matter." I urge that it is also a "new beginning." One matter must end for another to begin. Alan Leo and other writers are indeed eloquent about the Sun's progression to an opposition with Saturn: "A very malefic influence. The native will suffer in health, will experience much opposition . . . the mind will tend to despair and will ever look on the dark side of things. Despondency and depression will assail him . . . the best attitude to this adverse opposition will be one of hope and calmness and the inner feelings that 'whatever *is,* is best'. *A very critical and memorable period.*" Goodness! Might the native die? Venus ruling the VIIIth is squared by the Moon and Pluto; there is this tension in the IVth! Think how many astrologers would have jumped the gun! Think how the native might have been counseled in an earlier time!

The native was the picture of health. His modern company had prescribed continual medical checkups. There **was** hidden anxiety; that was why he was led to Astrology for counsel. But what does Saturn have to say in this horoscope? What is the architecture of advance for this man? A few questions about Saturn's first return to its birth position around thirty and transit of the Ascendant some six to seven years later would surely provide a clue.

In January, 1958, Saturn (with Mars) returned to the

Midheaven. Surely he had made a decision of ambition that would mold his next seven or fifteen years, a change in the way of professional self-application. He *had:* he had gone into the advertising business in New York City. There would have been a peak and some kind of beginning of an obscure period when Saturn came to the Ascendant in spring and fall, 1964. There was: he was promoted and sent abroad to the agency office in Germany. Did this foreign relocation somehow put the native out of sight, figuratively, of the intense business pressure of New York City? Did it bring him closer to himself (Pisces Ascendant, the important Neptune, mutable Signs on the angles; Saturn going to the Sun below the horizon)?

The advertising profession is clear: Jupiter ruling the Midheaven Sagittarius, Sign of big ideas, published programs, in conjunction with Mercury, communications, trine Neptune in the VIth, a kind of message creativity and creative camouflage; the Sun in Venus' Taurus, sharing a part of the IIIrd House of communications where we find the North Node in Gemini; the public pull and demand from Moon-Pluto in square to Venus—the only "hard" aspect in the horoscope. And there are other indices.

But the rising Mars is weak in Pisces. The Martian fire smoulders in the Piscean "wash." The stationary Neptune (as ruler of Pisces) focuses this mutation upon the work situation (VIth) where it works well (trine with Jupiter-Mercury), but is something other than it appears (Neptune). There is a muted aesthetic here that clashes, that struggles within the personality (Moon-Pluto square Venus). A simple question about this brought the revelation that the native had at one time wanted to be a painter and, indeed, had never stopped painting throughout his business career, but that income from a business career "demanded his time."

As the native talked about his views on art, his identity spoke directly. No bureaucratic frame filtered his inspiration (note the Fire emphasis throughout the horoscope). The Sun was in parallel with Neptune. The life energy wanted to build (Taurus) upon the highly personalized aesthetic. Was this the new beginning? Saturn was presenting a new plan, "commanding" his time. The Sun was to "begin again." Second adolescence again saw identity's ambition face to face. Mars had progressed into Aries and was in exact conjunction with the important radix Venus. Progressed Jupiter was nearing the radix Sun. Progressed Venus was on the North Node. The progressed Moon was nearing the Ascendant. Everything spoke of vitally fired aesthetic energy, increasing good fortune, aesthetic communication, a shift in personality and views. Could he—*should* he "suffer and despair" under this "very malefic influence" seen by Alan Leo in the progressed Sun opposing Saturn, the Saturn transit of the IVth cusp opposing its birth position? Should the native—who said he had "outgrown his position in the company and would be transferred"—go back to New York City, the advertising Mecca, leaving the relative obscurity of a foreign office, the isolation of language barriers and calmer ways? Or should he follow a new architecture of advance?

The native prepared his approach, resigned from his company with much good will and financial reward, and dedicated his life to building his art talent. Within five months, he developed a new art technique that, viewed privately by critics and buyers upon the international scene, caused considerable excitement and anticipation. The native lost weight and gained an infectious *joie de vivre*—his whole system, his identity was working efficiently. Preparation and modern times allowed a monumental shift in identity expression and rewarded it. Saturn's call provided the lure to his new life.

Astrologers can say that this is an exceptional case. The oldtimers, seeing the whole, might have flipped the switch from negative response to positive initiative and given this native the courage to be. But the frustrations might have taken different forms if society and social resources didn't applaud the refinement of individuality.. In this day and age, a man forty-five *can* change totally. Society now admires this courage. Astrologers should be aware always of the enormous potentials each identity has *in relation to the world in which it lives.* Our purpose is to share this awareness with our clients. Each case, each identity *is* exceptional.

Undoubtedly, astrologers deal more with women than with men. Women are more idle as a rule and have fewer opportunities to fulfill themselves, after giving birth and maintaining a house. In fact, the modern women's liberation movement is constructed to change the situation, to give women a more defined, flexed identity. The two examples we have studied cursorily are talented men at work in the world. They have opportunities every day to test themselves, to measure development, to draw acclaim and criticism. What about women? What does Saturn design for the housewife?

The question is more difficult than it sounds. It seems that, for the housewife, Saturn's meanings often reflect the ambition and structural changes of the husband, just as for a child Saturn reflects the family, the father. As soon as the housewife or unmarried woman has a job, a profession, Saturn's designs appear directly linked to her own professional progress. For an unemployed housewife, the call of Saturn doesn't disappear. It may be transferred to someone else or create a structure of effort in another dimension of life: the housewife may become a seeker after social status, for example, a club woman, a hobbyist, or charity worker. The institution of marriage and the home usually doesn't allow the housewife to flex her Saturn muscle to bring her own identity to full growth. This is a kind of circumstantial restriction and environmental press that can frustrate. The Saturn call is muted, displaced, and falls too easily into the classic meanings of the "lower Saturn level," the constrictions, sadness, coldness. The housewife cannot easily enjoy the expanded opportunities of self-realization in this modern time. This is the situation in which men as well as women found themselves years and centuries ago. The man inherited his job or trade from his father, whether he liked it or not. He stayed close to home and toed the governmental marks. What happened to the plant reaching for the Sun? What happened to the energy? Perhaps it was hidden, mutated. It wasn't released so it caused trouble. Saturn took the blame.

The example on page 32 again shows Saturn at the Midheaven in Sagittarius, immediately bringing the higher mind, education, religion, foreign countries into possible consideration (IXth House). Saturn is sextiled by the Moon in Saturn's Sign of exaltation, Libra, in the VIIth. We would expect a dignified, outwardly peaceful, serious personality presented to the public. It is immediately clear that Saturn receives and makes no other major "connection" with any other body, and that all the other "forces" are below the horizon. Saturn is in square to the Ascendant, which would suggest that its potential to lead the personality to development is not efficiently harnessed, frustrates the identity and may bring radical changes.

Uranus—the potential for individuation—nearest to rising, is squared by the Sun (life energy), Venus (aesthetic, sociability), and the retrograde Mercury (the mind, nervous system) all in Cancer (emotions, the home). These aspects corroborate our deductions from the Saturn position and the aspects to the Moon and Ascendant. There is a nervous anxiety about individual fulfillment, all held tensely "below the surface."

Mars and Jupiter are in conjunction, in sextile with the Sun, and trine to Neptune in the VIth. The native definitely would have expansive energetic thoughts about employment possibilities for her personality projection (Jupiter and Neptune are co-rulers of the Ascendant). But with Neptune involved from

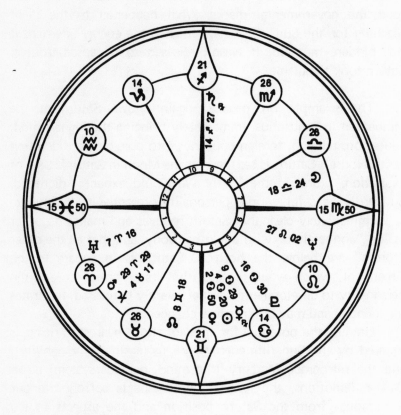

the VIth, whatever position she has isn't what it seems—her positions of service, her sense of duty. Here perhaps are plans without an architect. Pluto, also in Cancer and in the Vth (creativity, children, teaching) is squared by the Moon. The personality may want desperately to make a public presentation through teaching children, sharing her possibly unusual work ideas with the public, but self-leadership is missing. Saturn is not "connected" and Saturn rules Capricorn on the XIth, hopes and wishes.

The native came to this astrologer four months before her forty-third birthday. Immediately, we know that Saturn was approaching the opposition to its birth position, the time for a kind of second adolescence. The position would bring the opposition very near to the IVth cusp—another new beginning?

The native stated that her purpose for having the horoscope done was to find out what to make of her "religious feelings." She was really asking about IXth House affairs, how to bring Saturn's structure to the very personal and hard-to-understand feelings she had about her personal identity (Jupiter-Mars trine Neptune, involving the Ascendant through co-rulership; the sextiles to the Sun; Saturn's square to the Ascendant, sextile from the Moon).

A simple question about teaching revealed that the native had indeed been a teacher and had stopped to give birth to children—around twenty-eight to thirty, when Saturn returned to its position the first time, when a housewife-professional might change directions and become a mother and housewife exclusively? Yes. With such a Midheaven Saturn, we could expect a sudden marriage perhaps at the closing square to its birth position around twenty-one, conjunct the VIIth cusp (House of marriage, with the Moon ruling her Sun Sign Cancer; in Libra). (Note: especially since Uranus, by axial rotation would have risen to conjunction with the Ascendant at the same time.) Marriage had indeed occurred suddenly at twenty-two, when Saturn was transiting the VIIth cusp for most of 1950.

Saturn's rise to the Midheaven then saw the native traveling and teaching and growing. Saturn's return changed the way, new duties called, motherhood and the home took over. At the same time, the Sun progressed into Leo, in the Vth, children. This progressed position in Leo brought love and maturity and children strongly into the identity's development. It also made social prestige and personal authority important in the growing personality. The native became a social leader, holding office in social groups.

Saturn (with Mars) came to the Ascendant early in 1966, just before the native was thirty-eight years old. At the same time, the progressed Sun entered the VIth House (work, service). The native, evolving in stature, was suffering under inactivity. The structure couldn't complete itself, and Saturn's call was to build again toward bloom in later life. Children and the home were much less demanding with the time that had passed. The identity was again seeking plan and direction.

When the native spoke with this astrologer, she was considering a return to teaching: the progressed Moon was conjunct her radical Jupiter, involving the conjunction with Mars (energy), the sextile with the Sun, the trine with Neptune, the Ascendant through the rulerships, and the professional Xth in Sagittarius. Surely, this time was the beginning of a new plan, a repeat bid for identity structure.

The second stage could be anticipated with Saturn's transit in opposition to its birth position in July, 1972, and conjunct (stationary) the IVth cusp, to "new release," in October, 1972, and again in June, 1973. The "adolescence" recognition might set the stage for the final release.

At the same time, it must be noted that Uranus (sharp individuation) would transit the public Moon in January and October, 1972. Might the intensification of ambition press the native too soon into a new beginning and draw sharp public criticism? The native happened to be married to a prominent businessman, who was also importantly involved with the school at which she would work. Her admirable ambition would rock the social boat. Ambition always does. Might patience be better, or perhaps a more peripheral job in the school, still more attention devoted to problems at home, more prudent preparation (Saturn) before release would be *complete* in June, 1973, when the husband's work could very well take the family back to the United States? Would this final release, so much more dynamic and synthesizing of all the life's dimensions, really be the better goal in time?

The native became fascinated with her renewed self-awareness. Her style of dress changed, her habits, her views. She identified with those much younger. She accepted a full teaching job in September, 1971, espoused a most radical teaching method, and became deeply involved in a community uprising against her method and participation in the school. She endured, thanks to her inner pride (progressed Sun in Leo; Moon-Saturn sextile) and social balance (Moon in Libra in the VIIth), but lost much public prestige. She will repeat a second school year and leave the country—final release—in June, 1973. With careful planning, part of her individuation dream will be fulfilled when Saturn reaches the Sun in the fall of 1973 and again in the spring of 1974.

There is a threatening problem with her own child that may come to a focus at these same times (Moon square Pluto in the Vth). But the progressed Sun in trine to the radix Saturn is the native's first real link with Saturn in her life. She is holding tightly to her plan as it is—partly released—with a fixed nobility. Her services (VI) to herself, to her children, and to Saturn's larger plan and responsibilities are different than they appear (Neptune). With the first feeling of togetherness with Saturn in her life's energy organization, she chooses to stand alone.

In a real sense, a woman's position in the scheme of things is very demanding. Her identity reflects her husband's, her children's, her home's. But what about the woman's own identity? The demand upon the astrologer to interpret Saturn's call within modern opportunities for women is great. Husband, wife, children—and astrologer?—should work together to recognize the integrity and identity of the female.

The female's all too common position out of the stream of life sometimes makes expression of identity dimensions, the aspects in the horoscope, difficult. For example, it's not hard to come across horoscopes with the Sun opposing or squaring Neptune, easily involving Mercury as well. This can occur in about three periods every year; trines and conjunctions, in another three periods every year. Astrologers' files probably contain a disproportionate number of these cases because of the difficult challenge such aspects place upon the identity without adequate outlet for expression and development. With Neptune, the life energy exists with fantasy, perhaps some form of deception, perhaps some kind of highly evolved ecstasy. The artist can find an outlet. But what can happen if the native just does the laundry on Monday, cleans house on Friday, etc.? The dream world may be very rewarding. The sex life may have enough creativity in it to be outlet enough (or it may be problematic). Of course, it depends on the House and Sign positions of the Sun and Neptune, the architectural timing and structure of Saturn, and the other planets; but the point is to show the difficulty of self-relaization for women in most cases.

An example: Sun conjunct retrograde Mercury in Pisces in the IInd House opposing retrograde Neptune in Virgo in the VIIIth. This opposition axis keeps all other bodies below it. The woman has great potential with a VIIth House Moon trine the Sun, trine Mercury, sextile Venus, sextile Mars, square Saturn near the IVth cusp, square Jupiter, sextile Uranus, sextile Neptune. But the fantasy world has substituted for an incredibly passive husband and his encouragement of her. Her Capricorn Ascendant simply has been blotted out and a self-deception has taken over. Both man and wife live together, matching wits and sharing courtesies. There is no sex contact. They care for their children and present a truly amicable image.

When the progressed Sun came to the radical Saturn, the Capricorn Ascendant was awakened, and the native with dignity *and* authority planned to leave her husband, not for divorce, but to live alone in another country with the children and her fantasies. This astrologer suggested contemplation of separation only *after* a professional job and business exposure were attained by the wife. The horoscope shows the great need to be busy, creatively realized, and socially rewarded. Improved self-esteem would improve the ability to relate. These psychodynamic considerations are not related to our Saturn points in this chapter, but the burden upon a woman is illustrated with this short example.

Knowledge of the Saturn period can make drama out of routine newspaper and magazine stories. For example: just now, while writing these pages, I quickly scanned three consecutive daily newspapers and three weekly magazines. With keen awareness of the Saturn period, I always read news stories and obituaries of the famous for descriptions of what happened at fourteen to sixteen, especially, at twenty-eight to thirty, thirty-four to thirty-six, forty-five, sixty, ninety. Of course, news stories rarely provide more than the age. But matching ages and events in the lives of the unknown, the famous, the suffering, and the glorying indicates the drama of the identity, the reinforcement or disruption of the architecture of advance, and exercises our mind and observation in hypothetical construction of the horoscope. We share in the moment of news the focus of the identity in its development in time. Here are some random examples, from the last three days' news:

- 15 June 1972 (IHT), "Encore Concert—60 Years Later." Leopold Stokowski was celebrating his ninetieth birthday with a performance of the same concert program he had conducted at a memorable occasion sixty years earlier—when he was thirty! He made news then and now with the same material! (And remember the enormous tribute paid Picasso on his ninetieth birthday. The periods were very clearly defined throughout the stories of his life.)
- Stokely Carmichael, the American black-militant leader, was interviewed in Conakry, Guinea. He had left the United States and daily headlines three years ago—at twenty-nine—changed his way of identity expression, married, and now studied the African revolution in relative obscurity.
- Oakland, California, 18 June 1972 (AP)—"A twenty-one-year-old man about to begin serving consecutive life terms for a double murder conviction was married yesterday by the judge who sentenced him." What will happen when, in seven or eight years, Saturn makes the return to its birth position?
- The Angela Davis trial ended. The build-up of Saturn's return over the past twenty months—the length of arraignment and trial—climaxed for the twenty-eight-year-old black activist, and she is now touring the world with a new message, a new way, a new identity structure.
- A story about Muhammed Ali, the famous boxer and ex-heavyweight champion. What will the defeat by Frazier really mean in Ali's life? Is the rematch necessary? He is now twenty-nine years old.
- Georg Von Berkesy's obituary reveals that he won the Nobel Prize for research on ear mechanisms at sixty-one.
- Sirhan Sirhan's 1969 conviction for the assassination of

Robert Kennedy was modified to life imprisonment, 16 June 1972—ninety-five days before Saturn returned to its birth position in the horoscope of the twenty-eight-year-old.

- *Time* Magazine, 19 June 1972: "Elvis is back after 15 years." The rock-and-roll singer, movie-star was the public rage fifteen years ago at twenty-one to twenty-two. Now at thirty-six to thirty-seven, he's back and, in his own words, "I'm still the same." (He is divorcing his twenty-seven-year-old wife.)

- Ulrike Meinhof, at thirty-four to thirty-five, left her husband and children to lead the Red Army Faction of terrorists in West Germany.

- Always news about the Beatles. The world-famous music group disintegrated as each of the four became thirty. Each individual's way changed so dramatically, they couldn't stay together. Note how so many partnerships—and popular music groups—break up, if organized before twenty-eight to thirty, when Saturn returns to its birth position in the lives of the individuals involved.

- Education: A husband and wife, both twenty-nine, will become president and vice-president of Bennington College (Vermont) this week.

The list is endless, day after day after day: the chess whiz, Bobby Fischer is precisely at the zenith of his life, at twenty-nine. The defending champion Boris Spassky is thirty-five. Note the ages of conspirators in the rash of airplane hijackings!

Every person has his own personal drama. Fulfillment of potentials is the goal of life. The famous become so because they seem to fulfill more of their special potentials in tune with the expectations of the time and the masses. We learn much about the usual by observing the specialized.

Saturn in the Signs

So much has been written, so eloquently and sensitively, about Saturn in the Signs that the author cannot presume to elaborate significantly. But the objective of this book is to work with up-to-date case studies, showing modern reactions to eternally repetitive demands (Saturn) within modern opportunities and understanding; to show a wholeness of identity against the background of an ever-expanding and enormously diversified socio-time scheme; an identity that can be captured, felt, seen, appreciated "at a glance." The horoscope presents the immensity of the birth moment to our eye. Identities meet in an instant; perhaps the horoscope is less of a chore to understand (a myriad number of measurements) when we "feel" the whole structured in modern time and interpret with knowledgeable abbreviation.

The descriptions that follow abbreviate in a way that recognizes modern challenges and needs. The many writings known to us all elaborate beautifully for the most part. The many potentials of expression are invariably grounded to the following keys, which help to quicken recognition of the key to identity's ambition.

Saturn in Aries: open self-defensive mode for ambition

Saturn in Taurus: conservative building of ambition's plans

Saturn in Gemini: adaptable ambition; keen perception en route

Saturn in Cancer: deep need for encouragement of ambition; perhaps not received in early homelife

Saturn in Leo: ambition needs acclaim, uses dramatic techniques; the means more important than the end

Saturn in Virgo: hard-working ambition, easily bogged down with details

Saturn in Libra: ambition well balanced or modified by social awareness

Saturn in Scorpio: deepest working of self-organization; ambition carries complex defenses with it

Saturn in Sagittarius: high-minded ambition; direct and ethical manifestation

Saturn in Capricorn: strong, structural ambition; careful strategy

Saturn in Aquarius: social projection of ambition for unique service, opportunity, and endorsement

Saturn in Pisces: inner battle to distill ambition's true character and direction

It is very important to note that, while Saturn spends about two-and-a-half years in each Sign, it often makes aspects to the superior planets Uranus, Neptune, and Pluto for rather long periods of time, *affecting many, many births and subgenerations.* For example, the opposition between Saturn and Neptune from mid-1935 until early 1937 in Pisces and Virgo, respectively, seems to mute, to camouflage ambition, "put it to sleep." This doesn't mean that identities with this opposition have no drive or edge or thrust or endurance. Rather, Saturn in Pisces would have a more defined need for an inner battle to distill ambition's true character and direction. The challenge is reinforced; introspection can mold a more thought-out, more personal, more detailed application of ambition.

The Saturn conjunction with Pluto in Leo has been described already on page 5. We hear so much about this generation born after World War II. The war is coincidental and perhaps situationally relevant, but it is the working out of this particular Saturn-Pluto aspect, this "call," that embodies the ambition of those born from late 1946 through 1948.

For those born in mid-1941 through 1942 and early 1943, the Saturn conjunction with Uranus tends to complicate individuation through the dilemma of practicality versus idealism or uniqueness, conservatism versus impulse, convention versus idiosyncracy.

The Saturn conjunction made by Mars, occurring every two years or so, intensifies the "call" and can easily highlight the firing of situations throughout development.

The squares between Saturn and the superior planets (and Mars) intensify the manifestation and translate "awareness" of the dimensions into pressure between them.

Saturn in the Houses

Level and gender cannot be deduced from the horoscope. Gender (and race) are important to tell us how opportunities and expectations might be delineated by sociological considerations. Level is a product of this sociology and the native's free will and reactions throughout life. Placement of Saturn in the Houses is an important hint to ambition's substance, prerequisites, and mode of reaction.

Man in society is known by his works. Ambition symbolized by Saturn leads him to work expression. The work itself carries disciplines with it that guide and demand conformity as a first step to opportunity for fulfillment. In a very real sense, Saturn symbolizes a sociological super-ego for each individual: the demands made through the regimen of established experiences within society that guide man to his best work.

Saturn in the Signs suggests the nature of an individual's ambition, and Saturn's House position suggests the kind of experiences and style of expression that surround fulfillment of ambition. The experiences expected from Saturn's House position organize and adjust expression of ambition.

Saturn in an Angle will manifest itself most actively: the individual will express the ambition symbolism obviously, perhaps forcefully, depending upon support aspects elsewhere in the horoscope. Saturn in Cadent Houses suggests a less active state of affairs in ambition's expression: needs are expressed within developmental experience, and these needs must be met before ambition is activated within behavior. Saturn in Succedent Houses symbolizes ambition gaining expression through reaction, absorption, distribution: ambition here is more flexible, more eclectic, more malleable within society's prescriptions.

Saturn is a vital key to the understanding of man's work within his society, his projection of self-image in terms of building life development toward fulfillment within time. The following abbreviated observations will help us to clarify our vision and speed our understanding of an identity's architectural style and substance in terms of ambition.

Saturn in I: Serious personality, early responsibilities, lack of humor

Example 1: Retrograde Saturn in Sagittarius, seven degrees below the Ascendant, the only body in the eastern half of the horoscope (the "bucket" formation): the native is high-minded indeed, almost ministerial in his direct and ethical manifestation of ambition. His ambition rules his personality. Saturn rules Capricorn on the IInd, Aquarius intercepted there, and receives an opposition only from Venus in the VIIth: the native has risen to the height of the banking profession, leads church activities, is on school boards, adores philosophy, has suffered a broken marriage simultaneously with his tremendous, most recent promotion, when Saturn transited the IVth cusp conjunct the radical Uranus at age thirty-seven.

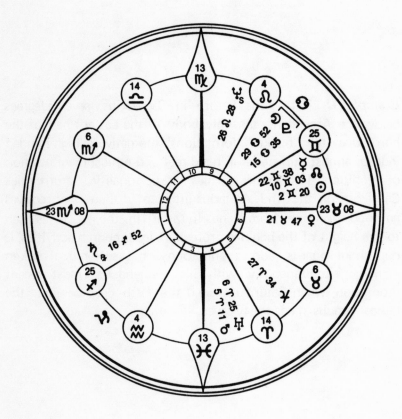

Example 2: Retrograde Saturn in Sagittarius in the Ist House, twenty-three degrees below the Scorpio Ascendant, the only body in the eastern half of the horoscope (again the "bucket"). The only close Saturn aspect is an opposition from Mercury in the VIIth where the Sun is. The native is a tall, ministerial symphonic and opera conductor. He is extremely interested in transcendental religious thought (Moon and Pluto in the VIIIth). His ambition is to bring structure to music and to communicate, through structure, a personal aesthetic to the public (but rarely, if ever, through a comic opera!).

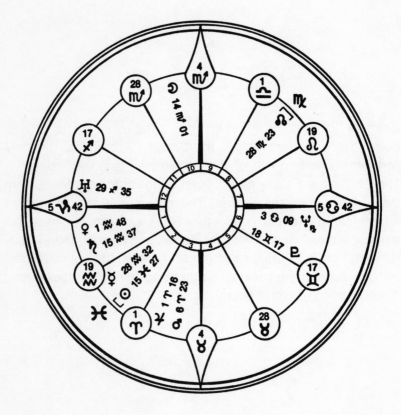

Example 3: Capricorn Ascendant, Saturn in Aquarius, nearing the IInd House where Mercury and the Sun are posited. This oft-married woman from the Rocky Mountain region "wears the trousers" in any group (and only her Sun, Moon, and Neptune are in feminine Signs). She is a sharp and stern funds-manager (Mercury and Sun in the IInd) and stands for no nonsense in any relationship (Moon in Scorpio in the Xth, ruling the VIIth; powerful Mars). But, with Venus rising in Aquarius, she is curiously delightful, refreshing, and valued for her talents and manner.

Saturn in II: Carefully built resources, structure

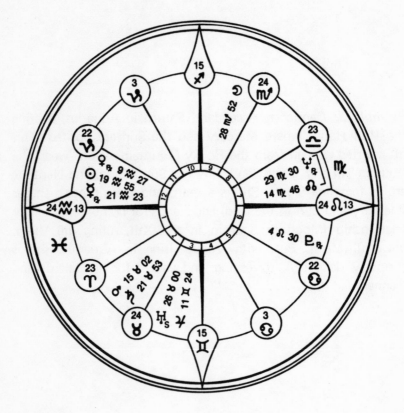

Example 4: This businessman has Saturn and Mars together in Taurus in the IInd, squared by the Sun and Mercury in the XIIth near the Aquarius Ascendant. The native is intensively cautious about the structuring of his bureaucratic talent. There is an ever-present tension about applying *his* plan (highly individualistic, with Uranus five degrees past Saturn, also squared by the Sun, ruling the Ascendant and Sun Sign, posited in the IIIrd) within the large corporate structures where he is employed. He works hard to get his ambition into phase with institutional development. He often wears himself out by feeling indispensable.

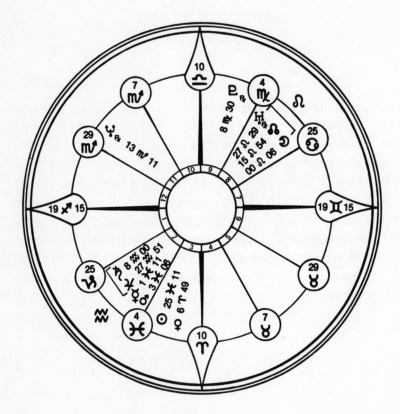

Example 5: This young girl, as soon as she started school at six, seized every opportunity to project herself upon the organization of her classmates and parlay opportunities into financial (!) profit. She conjured up precocious financial "empires." Extraordinarily bright, she was the first to volunteer for and dramatize any group activity. Further corroboration: Saturn in Aquarius with Jupiter and Mercury-Mars conjunction in Pisces in the IInd; Sun and the Aries-Venus in the IIIrd; Sagittarius Ascendant.

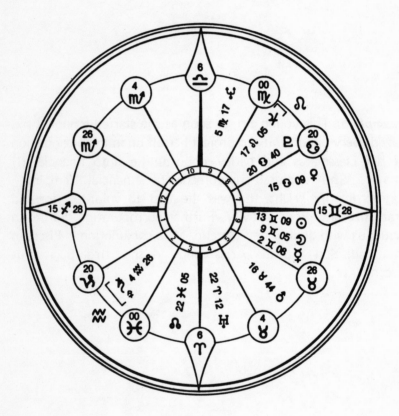

Example 6: Retrograde Saturn in Aquarius intercepted in the Capricorn IInd, the only body in the eastern half of the horoscope (but not the "bucket" formation since Saturn shares no opposition to focus its position). The native is keenly aware of the need for cautious management of his inheritance. Decisions are very difficult for him (New-Moon birth in Gemini with Mercury, in the VIth; the trine to Saturn from the VIth helps find focus, but still, grounding is lacking). He builds conscientiously within partially inherited structures, and his ambition always is seeking anchor and security.

Saturn in III: Easily depressed, highly mental response

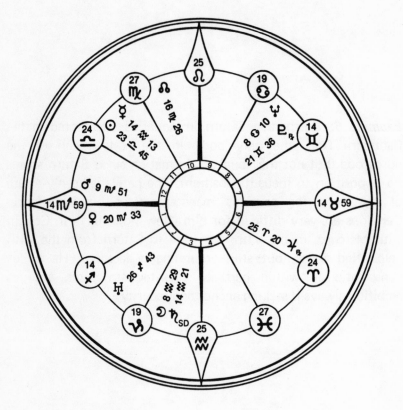

Example 7: Stationary Saturn in Aquarius, six degrees ahead of the Moon, both in the IIIrd, squared by Mars in the XIIth just above the Scorpio Ascendant and Venus just below. This voice-teacher is known for his "inspired" and classically academic deductions about voice production and music interpretation. As Saturn transited the "obscure" quadrant, on its second return to its birth position near the IVth cusp, approaching sixty years, the native had powerful depressions about "having been bypassed by time." His own personal worries were difficult restrictions and he sought almost mystical, deeply soul-searching rationalizations: "I'm born in the wrong century." Saturn's return did wonders, and the identity seized numerous new opportunities for his unique service. Endorsements abounded.

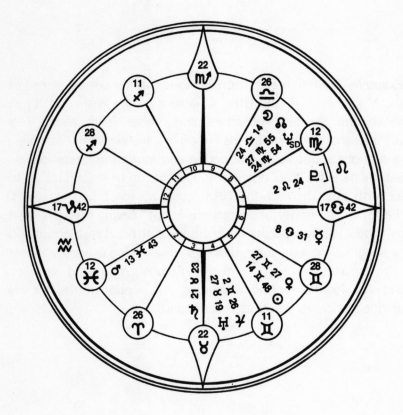

Example 8: With Saturn in Taurus practically conjunct the IVth cusp, this sociologist-teacher-writer waited patiently through the "obscure" period, building a plan for his ambition upon Saturn's first return: he wrote and lectured voluminously (Mercury in the VIth and Pluto in the VIIth) and surmounted difficulties in his home as Saturn returned. His building paid off in a university appointment. His tension is always absorbed mentally, causes headaches, and yet stimulates further writing and academic profit in this extremely creative and artistic Gemini (Sun in the Vth square Mars in Pisces in the IInd).

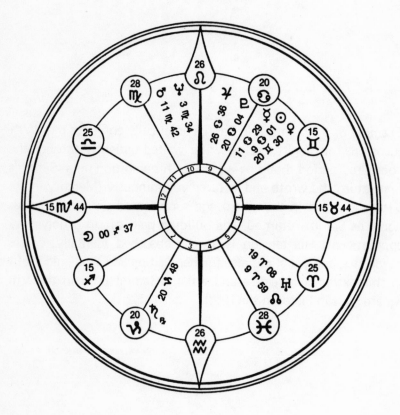

Example 9: Retrograde Saturn in Capricorn on the cusp of the IIIrd, opposed by Mercury, Pluto, and Jupiter in Cancer on the IXth cusp. The native was a stockholder (Jupiter rules the IInd; Venus is sextile Uranus in the Vth, from the VIIIth, other people's resources). He built strong, powerful, very individual speculations with much profit (Saturn opposition axis squared by Uranus). Yet, he couldn't fit the organization of bureaucracy. His mood fluctuations are powerful as times of inspiration (Moon in the Ist square Mars and Neptune in the Xth). Finally, as Saturn came to the VIIth cusp, he structured a new public presentation by organizing a school for children with mental problems, on the grounds of his large home.

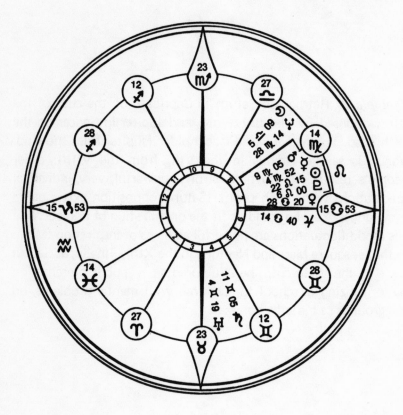

Example 10: A stellium in the VIIth within the Signs Cancer, Leo, and Virgo; Neptune and the Moon in the VIIIth. Saturn-Uranus are in Gemini in the IVth, squared by Mercury and Mars. The native has had to adapt his ambition frequently to home and environment—the dilemma being the conflict between conventionality and impulsive, unusual ambitions (Saturn conjunct Uranus in double-bodied Gemini). His father is extremely sick. The native suffered acute family embarrassment from failing his college examinations when Saturn came to the Ascendant, then opposed the stellium. He has developed a precocious maturity and consciously nurtured patience with himself despite nervous tension. Saturn's return will bring a new beginning, probably a return to the father, the homeland, through cooperation in business or inheritance. The native is an accountant with much interest in drama and theatricality (Sun and Pluto in Leo; Moon-Neptune conjunction; Saturn conjunct Uranus; VIIth House emphasis).

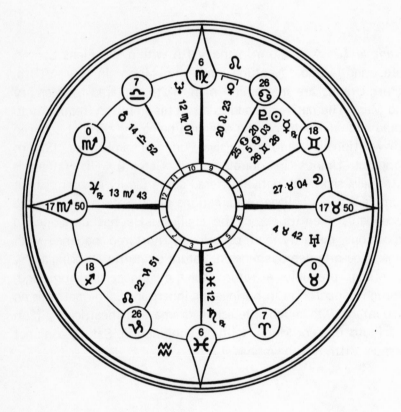

Example 11: The IVth House retrograde Saturn in Pisces, opposing Neptune, trined by the Cancer Sun in the VIIIth and the retrograde Jupiter in Scorpio, just above the Ascendant in the XIIth. She is a university mathematics teacher who appears much older than she is. The Grand Trine encourages a closed circuit emotionally, centered upon early home concerns, involving mother and brother (Saturn rules the Signs on the IIIrd). Money has been squandered upon the shiftless brother (retrograde Jupiter trine retrograde Saturn from the XIIth); her emotional caring soothes the home but frustrates her own battle to distill personal ambition, true character, and direction. Her personal ambitions are temporarily asleep until the home situation settles itself.

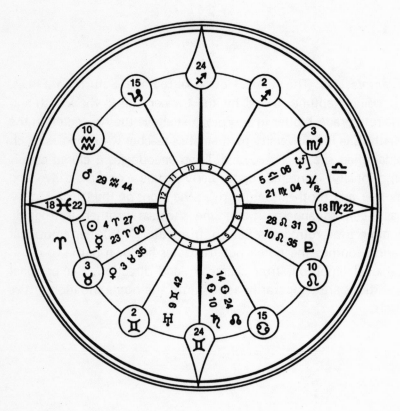

Example 12: This teacher has a Pisces Ascendant with the Sun intercepted in Aries, opposing Neptune in the VIIth, both squared by the IVth House Saturn in Cancer. A passive father and much home relocation deprived the native of the encouragement her energies sought. Aries' fire smouldered. A play-acting (Neptune) maturity brought her image to the public. Patience in time has indeed overcome impulse. Often, an out-and-out trickiness tries to attract the attention and encouragement needed so deeply.

**Saturn in V: Protection for self-giving;
Self-Defense; overly structured creativity, sexuality**

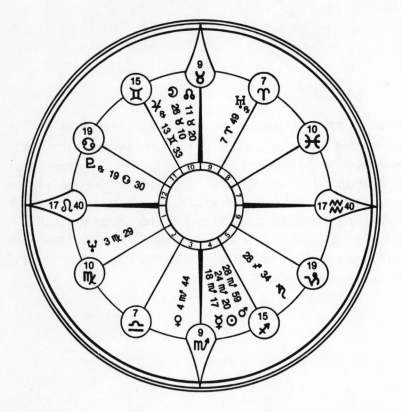

Example 13: Full-Moon birth with Venus, Mercury, Sun, and Mars in Scorpio in IV; Leo Ascendant. The Vth House Saturn in Sagittarius makes only wide aspects over the Sign line: trine to rising Neptune, a sextile from Venus, very wide square to Uranus in the IXth. This homosexual male has been "burned" many times, giving affections and creativity to those who have not fully appreciated the high level of his intentions, his high hopes for creative enterprise and personal relationship. He guards his personal giving and overstructures his creative work defensively, often to the point of deceiving himself (Neptune rising). Superb progressions into the Capricorn part of the Vth and a progressed New Moon are bringing him renewed self-esteem in his international art dealership.

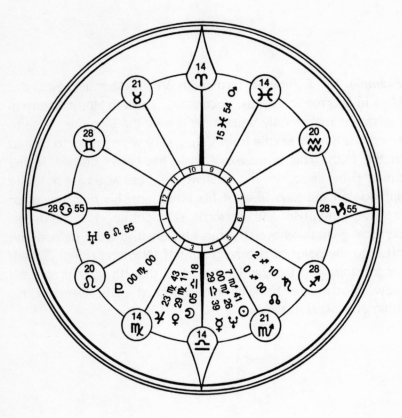

Example 14: This young girl seems to have had her early thoughts about personal ambition and identity development turned aside, possibly in the home. There is a Cancer Ascendant with Uranus in the Ist, Sun conjunct Neptune in Scorpio, with Mercury, in the IVth. The home may be different than it seems. Her adolescence-awareness (at Saturn's opposition to its birth position) was critical, with the Mars-Saturn conjunction transit in early Gemini, opposing the transiting Neptune which covered the radical Saturn. The young girl experiments widely with drugs, hides and defends her position painfully. She has found new structures for ambition and creativity through music and fantasies, without anchor in the home and parental perspective. She gave and was perhaps not accepted or heard.

Saturn in VI: Security sought in organization, a lack of open-minded flexibility

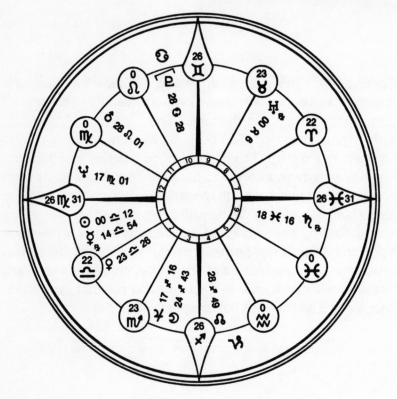

Example 15: Only Saturn and Uranus, both retrograde, are in the western half of the horoscope. The emphasis on ego here is strong with a Libra Sun four degrees below the Virgo Ascendant. The VIth House Saturn opposes a XIIth House Neptune, both squared by a Sagittarian Jupiter in the IIIrd with the Moon. Growing up, the native was part of two families through family and children friendship; a son in the friend family became her husband. The ego tried hard to define itself, to distill its true character and direction. She was a poor student and sought to organize others' activities as best she could. Professionally, she became successful as a librarian and, in marriage to a Pisces, she organizes everything and everybody. The opposition (awareness) with Neptune in the XIIth has helped her be aware of these narrowing tendencies in adult life, and it is a pleasure to watch her sociability and open-mindedness grow with development.

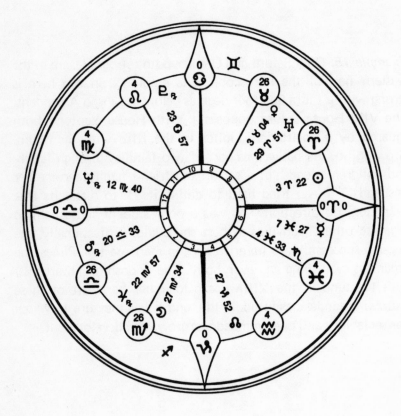

Example 16: Libra Ascendant; Aries Sun in the VIIth; Mercury conjunct Saturn in the VIth, opposing Neptune in the XIIth. The native presents an intense, fiery public image. She structures her life to an extreme, allowing her an at-home profession as music teacher (Venus conjunct Uranus in VIII; Pluto square the rising Mars, both retrograde, from the Cancer Midheaven, Moon conjunct retrograde Jupiter in the IIIrd). She fights hard to find her real identity and ambition in relation to her conductor husband and the public music positions they both share. Her inflexibility, with the frequent complaining about time that seems characteristic of VIth House Saturns, is a sex and home harmony problem (Saturn and Uranus rule the Aquarian Vth; and Saturn, the Capricorn IVth).

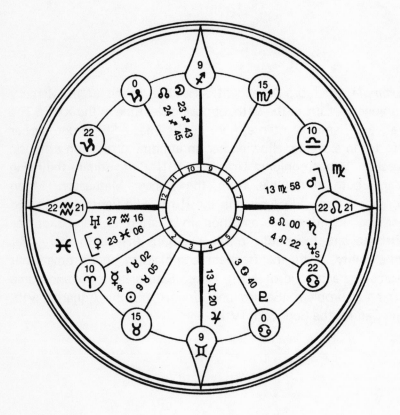

Example 17: This inventor has Uranus rising, five degrees below the Aquarian Ascendant and Venus nearby in Pisces. Saturn and a stationary Neptune are in conjunction in Leo in the VIth. The native's ambition demands acclaim and his work is indeed dramatic. He leaves the final promotion and manufacturing details to his powerful wife (Mars in Virgo in the VIIth). His ambition and talent are secure in her organization, which allows him enormous flexibility.

Saturn in VII: Learning through experience and interaction, importance of public and partners

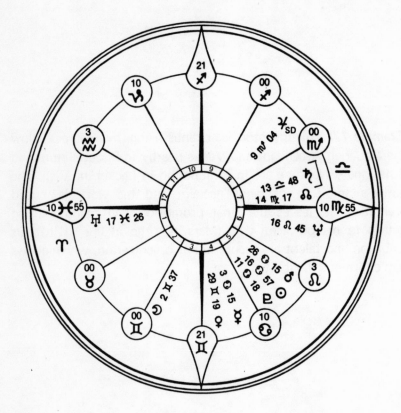

Example 18: This housewife, with a Pisces and intercepted Aries Ascendant, Uranus seven degrees below the horizon, wanted desperately to be a nurse (Pluto, Sun, and Mars in Cancer in the Vth). An accident prevented this dream, and she became a dietician instead (Neptune in the VIth, "substitution"; Sun square Saturn in the VIIth). Additionally, she married a doctor, ever trying to fulfill her ambition through her social interaction and public relationships. In many ways, she achieved for her ambition a good balance between the dream and the reality.

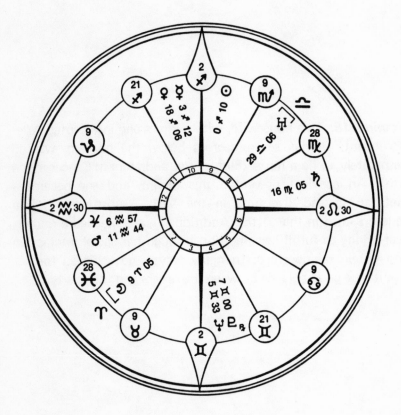

Example 19: Charles de Gaulle had a Virgo Saturn in the VIIth and a rising Jupiter-Mars in Aquarius. His hard-working ambition built a new France. His austere patience with details in fulfilling his way is legend. The Sun-Mercury-Venus conjunction in Sagittarius at the Midheaven, widely squaring Saturn, gave the severe, structurally simple, and brilliantly effective public communication of his personal designs for France. His Moon was in Aries in the IInd House in trine to the Midheaven group.

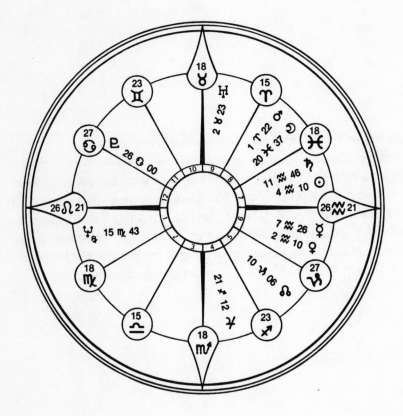

Example 20: The late Leo Ascendant holds the Virgo Neptune in the Ist House, opposed by the VIIth House Sun-Saturn-Moon conjunction in Pisces (the Moon into the VIIIth). The native is a teacher (Jupiter in Sagittarius at the Vth cusp, square both Neptune and the Moon, ruling Pisces). She has worked very hard to fulfill her own professional ambitions and maintain a family, supporting a Capricorn husband in his career as well. Her energetic interaction with so many publics has built a remarkable scope of experience for her. Mars in Aries trine a late Cancer Pluto in the XIth draws her energies ever further to new public experiences and hopes.

Saturn in VII: Search for self, caution with others

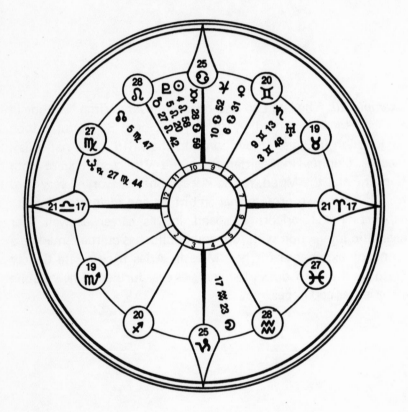

Example 21: The native has only the Moon under the horizon, in Aquarius in the IVth House, in wide opposition to Mars in the Xth. Saturn and Uranus are in conjunction in Gemini in the VIIIth. Neptune is on the cusp of the XIIth, and all the other bodies cluster at the Midheaven within fifty-one degrees. The native has much difficulty finding focus for her ambition—and constantly struggles between the conventional and the idiosyncratic to express herself. Her mental perceptions are keen and multiple to the extreme about many, many things. She searches for her identity almost mystically, while interrupted only by demands of the home. She is cautious with others because she intellectually knows her own self is not yet completely formed. Saturn's return and other factors opened a door to her, and through careful study of Astrology, she has found an ambitious new way to self-discovery and understanding of her observations of others.

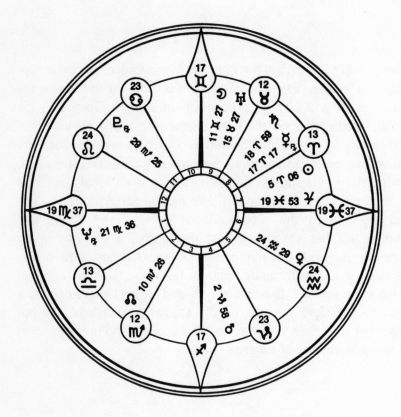

Example 22: The VIIIth House Saturn here is in conjunction in Aries with a retrograde Mercury, ruler of the Virgo Ascendant, Neptune rising. The Aries Sun in the VIIth gives the native an energetic public projection. He is an opera conductor and curiously apologetic that he doesn't really fit the fiery, dictatorial image expected of important conductors (Herbert von Karajan and Toscanini, Arians). He searches for a deeper understanding about himself by a deep, academic study of esoteric Astrology.

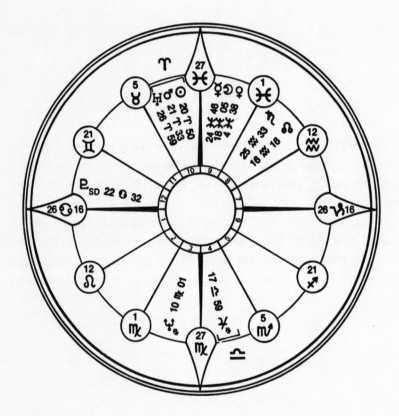

Example 23: Cancer Ascendant, Saturn in Aquarius in the VIIIth. The native has sought a social projection of his ambition for unique service in two countries (Moon, Venus, Mercury in Pisces in the IXth; Sun, Mars, Uranus in Aries in the Xth). The search has caused him to change homes and languages several times. He works to find himself, to the point of actually having changed national citizenship (Pluto nearly conjunct Ascendant, trined by the Moon and Mercury).

Saturn in IX: Judicial and righteous, foreign ambitions

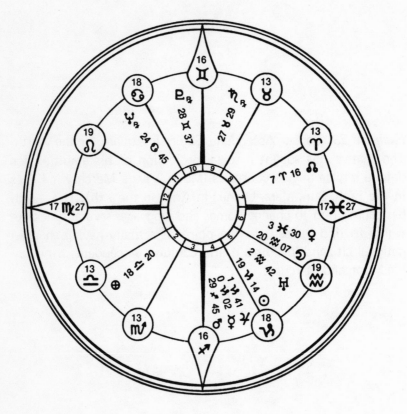

Example 24: On a very specialized level, President Nixon is a perfect example (see page 7) His Saturn in Taurus (retrograde) corresponds to his enormous conservatism and the patient building of this superb politician. His campaigns have always involved foreign affairs. His espousal of the judicious and righteous certainly are integral to his position on policy and his profession as a lawyer. The square between Saturn and the Aquarian Moon in the VIth, with Pluto in Gemini in the Xth, perhaps corresponds to the past criticisms of self-righteousness and "tricky" ambition in his work and campaigning styles. A powerful Capricorn. Saturn's transit of Neptune in opposition to the Sun must be watched carefully (spring, 1973, through Summer, 1975).

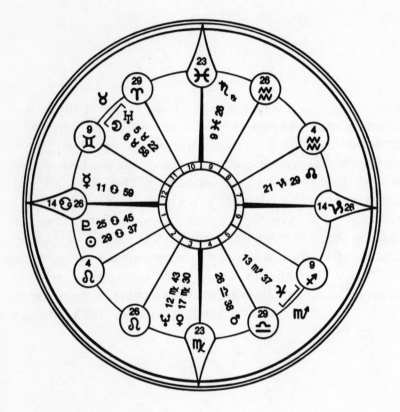

Example 25: This opera singer has a retrograde Saturn in the IXth in Pisces, opposing a Neptune-Venus conjunction in Virgo in the IIIrd. The native has worked hard to distill the true character and direction of his ambition. He wanted to be a minister. He became a businessman, unsuccessfully. He married two women of foreign extraction and lives now with his second wife in a foreign country. His ambition and personality took on the final identity change when Saturn made its first return.

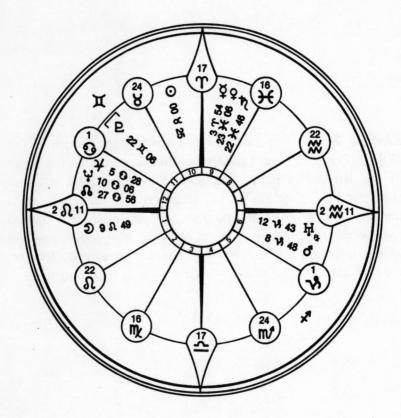

Example 26: With Saturn in very close conjunction with Venus in Pisces, and with Mercury in Aries, all in the IXth, this woman married a very judicial and righteous man, much older than she. He afforded her world-travel opportunities, fulfilling every dream and ambition she ever had for herself (Moon in Leo rising, trine Mercury).

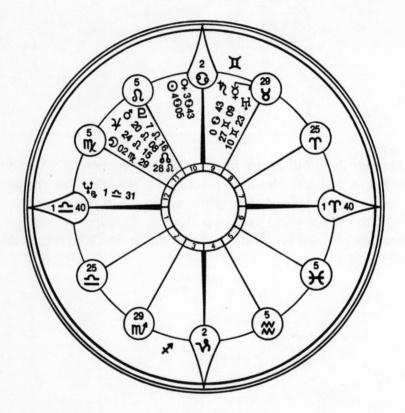

Saturn in X: Determination, early winner

Example 27: Neptune conjunct the Libra Ascendant, squared by the Saturn-Venus-Sun conjunction exactly on the Midheaven. Uranus and Mercury are intercepted in Gemini in the IXth, and Jupiter, Mars, and the North Node are in conjunction in Leo in the XIth, with Pluto and the Moon. This young woman was an international opera singer at an extremely early age. Her determination, talent, and the winning of one of the world's most important international contests have provided her Cancer Saturn with much needed encouragement; it was not really endorsed when so precociously shown in early homelife (father separated).

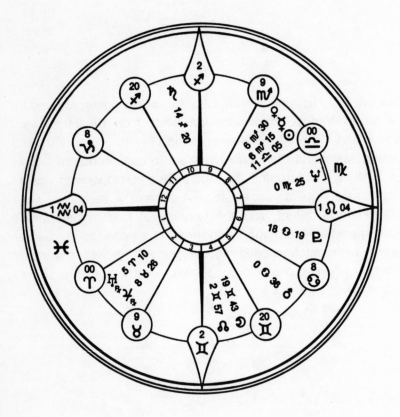

Example 28: With the Sagittarian Saturn in the Xth, opposed by a Gemini Moon on the cusp of the Vth, trine an VIIIth House Sun, this educator-writer-critic received awards and enormous publishing prestige early in his career. As Saturn and Mars transited the IVth cusp and North Lunar Node at age forty-three and a half, his position as an important international critic was further reinforced. In person, his personality is veiled and distant, almost secretive. His energy shines through his writing and public criticism.

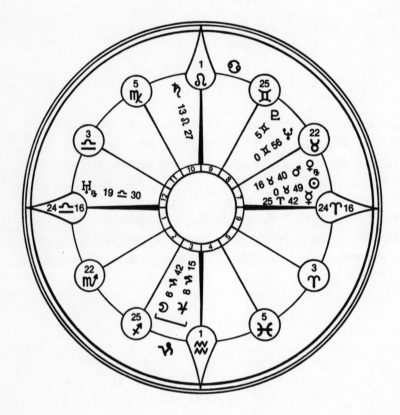

Example 29: This Xth House position of Saturn is often called the "Napoleon Saturn," not especially for the comparatively early achievement to which it corresponds, but perhaps more for the "fall" after achievement that has been noted as Saturn descends to the horizon and further to the IVth cusp. Indeed, Napoleon had this Saturn position in Cancer (deeply needing encouragement and acclamation because of his small stature?), and Hitler, as shown, had it in Leo (demanding acclaim for ambition, dramatic technique, ends lost sight of). The "falls" are less obvious in modern times. Capricorn J. Edgar Hoover certainly held onto his very early-won high post with the FBI (Saturn in Scorpio: the entire country and criminal justice organization was called into defense of his tenure and ambition at the close of his life). Understanding the timing of development helps to soften the onus of expected fall from this mighty position of Saturn.

Saturn in XI; Need for love and acceptance, popularity

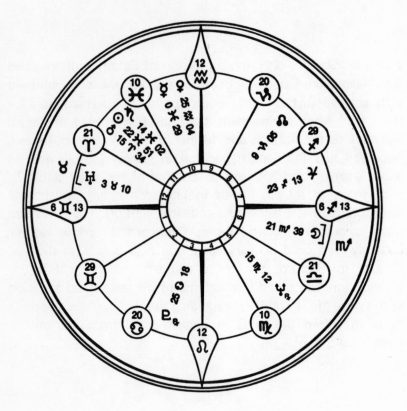

Example 30: Sun conjunct Saturn in Pisces, opposing Neptune retrograde in the Vth. There is also a Grand Trine in Water Signs among the Sun, Moon in Scorpio intercepted in the VIth, and Pluto retrograde in Cancer in the IIIrd. The native is a very glib, articulate, high-powered international salesman (Gemini Ascendant, Mercury in the Xth, Mars in Aries in the XIth). He is also extraordinarily involved in art collection. His creativity, his dreams are something other than they seem. He is extremely tied to the Grand Trine, its emotional closed circuit, need for public acceptance and material standards. When Saturn and Mars came to his Ascendant, he faced the challenge to distill the true character and direction of his ambition. He has been urged to settle his need for popularity with his art-museum dreams. (He has an adopted child.)

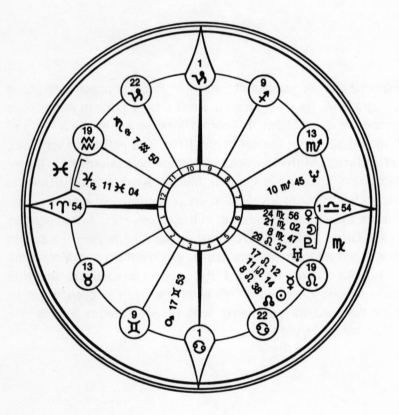

Example 31: This young lady has a retrograde Saturn in Aquarius in the XIth, opposed by the Sun in the Vth, with an Aries Ascendant. She is a forthright, energetic, and precociously responsible youngster. Her need for acceptance by her children friends is enormous. Her father is very influential upon her, and together they have created an understanding of social relationships and family love to help her project her ambition for and development of unique service in life. She often talks of becoming a teacher (Vth House and Moon emphasis).

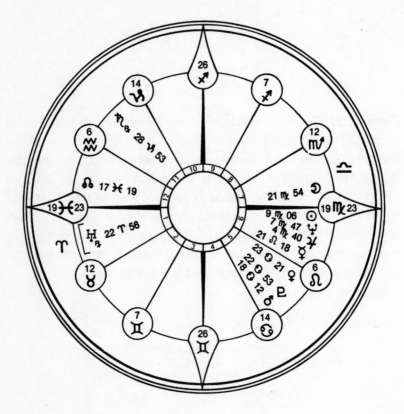

Example 32: Mars, Pluto, and Venus in Cancer conjunction in the Vth are in opposition to the XIth House Capricorn Saturn, retrograde. The axis is squared by an Arian Uranus, retrograde and intercepted in the Ist House with a Piscean Ascendant. The need for love and acceptance is crucial. It is the structure of the entire identity. The extremely subtle mental strategies involved are further indicated by the Jupiter, Neptune, Sun, and Moon cluster and wide conjunction in Virgo in the VIth. The man is desperately caught up in his work to gain the recognition he never got from his father, does not get from his wife, and barely gives himself.

Saturn in XII: Weak against restriction, needs leadership

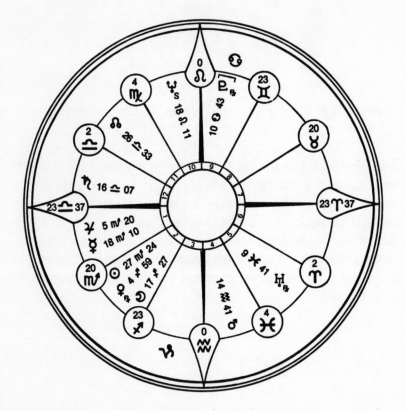

Example 33: The exalted Saturn in Libra in the XIIth, just above the Ascendant, trined by Mars in Aquarius in the IVth, sextile Neptune in the Xth and Moon in the IInd, is still weak against restrictions. Before authority in his business, the native has difficulty bending. His awareness of the need to develop a strategy of balance makes his ambition "hurt." He becomes his *own* enemy. To accept leadership has become this man's wisdom after he realized that his ambition would always "feel" restrained somehow. He does his important job superbly and with a creativity that brings much success (rising Jupiter-Mercury trine Uranus in the Vth). This Scorpio Sun shines brighter, now that it shines out instead of in.

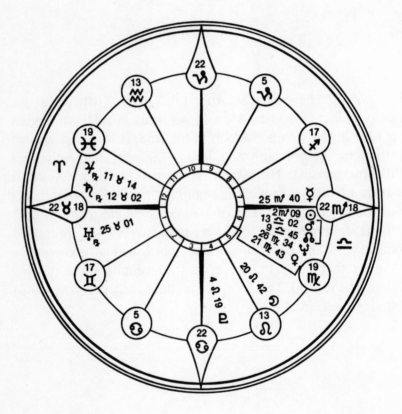

Example 34: Saturn and Jupiter are in conjunction in Taurus, both retrograde, the only bodies above the horizon. The Taurus Ascendant is highly powered by an exact opposition between Uranus rising and Mercury setting (Mercury in Scorpio). This housewife's Scorpio Sun, Libra Mars, and Virgo Venus and Neptune are all in the VIth House, the Sun square Pluto in the IVth, the Moon squaring the Uranus-Mercury axis from Leo in the Vth. Her ambition simply lies still. A nervous critical nature preoccupies her in all relationships. To give a compliment to someone curiously diminishes her. She's building something through her husband but has so many private, nervous restrictions that she can't externalize. She tends to criticize the leader before enjoying the leadership offered. The father had depressed every individuation effort for the first fifteen years, and at twenty, she ran away to momentary independence, getting married to her husband-leader (Taurus Sun) at twenty-two.

Among the famous, Saturn's House position is clearly understood since these public personalities externalize so much of their ambition: they have a much larger arena and are expected somehow to justify their goals and energies. Salvador Dali is making an obscurely personal statement of his search for self (Saturn in the VIIIth); the Duke of Windsor gave up the throne to find his life's and love's true identities (Saturn in the VIIIth); Alfried Krupp von Bohlen und Halbach inherited at a young age one of the world's mightiest personal empires from a long line of family power and watched his house of steel and munitions crumple in World War II (Saturn in the IVth); Marilyn Monroe's gruesome childhood gave her trauma as well as enormous self-identification for her ambitious rise (Saturn in IV); Handel's glorious creations and eternal architectonic music certainly show his Saturn in the IInd House (suggested by this astrologer's rectification). Stalin built his ambition into Russia's rise with a "ruthless" plan (Saturn probably in the IInd). Our example on page 19 achieved his social projection of ambition through religion, most determinedly, after having been an early winner in an entirely different public field. The native discussed on page 25 was finally able, with determination and early success, to find outlet for the ambition of his higher mind in a whole new phase of growth and development. The example on page 31 fulfilled the international potential by living abroad in different countries and the educational, high-minded ambitions by working in a school; the righteousness within social upheaval made fulfillment difficult.

The thirty-four examples above are only fragments focusing upon Saturn's position in the Houses as a key to further thought about the whole horoscope. The words are chosen carefully in hopes that the reader will be able to amplify them and grasp the identity in a glance. In the chapters that follow, these examples are frequently referred to in varying detail.

Retrogradation

We cannot be absolutely definitive about the identity correspondences with retrogradation since the phenomenon is apparent; i.e., there is no actual backward motion of the planets. The rotation of the earth as the planets make their turn in orbit, when viewed against the stationary projection of the Zodiac, causes us to see apparent backward movement. Yet, somehow retrogradation seems to register, and, in our many examples above, the word has come often into the descriptions.

It might be rewarding to consider that understanding retrogradation manifestation has less to do with apparent "backward" movement and more to do with the fact that the planet, after going direct again, will *cover the same ground over which it apparently back-tracked.* Painters and sculptors repeat certain accents in their works; symphonic form calls for repetition of important themes. Businesses publish annual reports to evaluate again the year already passed.

Saturn, for example, is retrograde for 140 days and stationary approximately five days before and after retrogradation. In the progressed horoscope, "days," of course, may be read as "years." Depending upon where in the retrograde period a native is born, there is a good chance, or no chance, that Saturn within a lifetime can re-assume direct motion. Of course, it does occur, and can be expected to occur with Mercury, Venus, Mars, and Jupiter with shorter periods of retrogradation.

If Saturn is to turn direct and cover the same ground again—speaking symbolically here—it stands to reason that Saturn would do so with knowledge of the ground already covered: the identity would have a direct and easier awareness of ambition during the direct period.

With a birth Saturn retrograde, there seems to be a counterpoint to ambition—not necessarily a "going away from" or a diffidence of any kind. The identity holds another "theme". or motive within the perspective and scope of its ambition.

Usually, it can be related to parental (father, or the mother as father-image) difficulty, undue pressure, avoidance, or family separation. Often the native can have internalized some inferiority feelings and, with growth, adopted a sense of superiority to overcompensate. Then, the native is vulnerable to exploitation, having his own ambition usurped to serve that of others, all in the name of identity reinforcement, feeling the self as important.

A few questions in this direction, tracking down a retrograde Saturn, invariably turn up very important considerations about the security, the "themes" of ambition.

With Mercury, the counterpoint is a mental parallel with reality, promising a reorientation, a shift in thought when direct motion is regained. With Venus, the counterpoint is within the emotions in the same way (more about this in the next chapter). With Mars, often particularly telling, the counterpoint to energy expenditure keeps much inside and, in the appropriate configurations, endangers the health and nervous system. With Jupiter, there can be a muted enthusiasm, a deep contentment with being alone, for example, and a shift or displacement of rewards.

In all cases, the shift to direct motion brings an important release in the progressed horoscope; the lapse into retrograde motion brings a corresponding shift into counterpoint, a new theme introduced to play against or with the major melody.

Saturn is the architect within time, early times and modern times. Identities today have infinitely more outlets and opportunities to adjust. Buildings are built higher, of different materials, last longer, and serve more purposes than ever before. The architect knows the purpose, the design, and the tolerances.

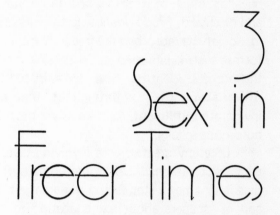

Sex in Freer Times

Sex is nothing new. But modern times have expanded the meaning, application and freedom of sexual energy. It is now an acknowledged joy, a potential problem, a powerful energy, a modern sedative. It is a goal and an escape. It reinforces the ego and can erase it. Sex, on the modern mind and in every identity's environment, is a vital psychological force in every life.

The first thing that identifies us with someone, during a moment of fleeting awareness or purposeful study, is usually something sexual. The expanded meaning of sex links creativity—artistic and biological as well as social—to this primal energy source. Sex was the key note of the pleasure which Freud said we seek to avoid pain. Yet, in the actual physical act of sex, we enjoy pleasure from the increase of tension. We delay release.

Sex is symbolic of social and individual freedom, espoused by the modern generation of young people (under thirty!). It is an argument now challenging the Catholic Church and over one thousand years of dogma. If sex really is a natural force, why have we not let it be natural up to now? Why have we confined sex within legal and religious forms?

Of course, the answer is that sex is really too natural and can

115

interrupt the sociological framework necessary for group activity and ordered population progress. But sex in modern times seems to have lost much of its threat now that it has been so acknowledged and discussed. Freud opened up the subconscious and released the id. Society has absorbed the freedom, molded the energies into new forms—even established political movements upon them—and, in the process, identities have disseminated the expansive, creative dimensions of sex throughout, that form the identity and invigorate fulfillment. As soon as sex must be discussed the *whole* horoscope speaks.

Like any creative area involving taste, style, technique, and personal preference, sex is the domain of considerable personal bias. Major news stories and research published in our magazines and newspapers about sex education reveal how many doctors are uninformed or embarrassed to give sex counsel to patients, how many patients are embarrassed to ask for help with a sex problem. Imagine how many astrologers are biased against understanding sex in the horoscope and discussing it with a client. Sex is too vitally important as a social and personal energy to be overlooked or soft-pedaled.

Today, in much of the Western world, pornography is immediately available for viewing and purchase. It is legalized in Denmark. But it is just as available in Germany and Missouri. Advertising is replete with outspoken sexual references and erotic overtones. Movies. Fiction. Contact clubs. —Man's imagination has taken what once was subliminal and projected it upon every facet of his identity expression.

Fourth graders learn about sex in schools. Artists have known it intimately as a kind of esoteric badge of their creative work. Politicians are concerned about their sex-appeal. Some parents band together to fight the wave of energy acknowledgement. (Perhaps this says something about the parents more than about the supposed moral nature of the times.)

Older Astrology and medical texts discuss masturbation as "self-pollution," as a cause of insanity. Some books show pictures of people debilitated by the "secret vice." This was not more than one or two generations ago! Today, we supposedly know better, and hundreds of sex books encourage the freedom of this and other sex expression. Men and women must address themselves to masturbation, premarital sex, sex techniques, abortion, and child sex education. They must know *their* own position—and respect it—before they can expect to guide their children or be comfortable in a social image. —The astrologer must be prepared to help with this vital modern reality. Each individual should have his sex profile in clear focus, for it influences the whole of the horoscope that is identity.

It is curious how one often expects all homosexuals to be effete or even identifiable, dancers or musicians to number more out-and-out sexualists in their ranks than other professional groupings. Might it be that the creative atmosphere in the art world uses more sexual energy, or uses the energy more openly than the business world? Sex is expressed in so many ways: from shaking hands, to appreciating a painting, to painting one, even to enjoying selling one; the sexual overtones of religious ecstasy are well known. We are talking about subjective reaction, emotional response, even chemical reaction. Things beautiful, charming, lovely, sensual, voluptuous; ugly, rude, slovenly, embarrassing—all really belong to the creative, subjective emotional responses contained in sex.

Stravinsky's *Rite of Spring* ballet is about emotional, physical rejoicing at the birth of new life under the Sun. Astrologers know the sensitive significance of the vernal equinox. Yet, there was a riot at the ballet's first performance. Astrologers have been maligned for such superstition. Is it perhaps that an artist in his vision—even an astrologer—may come too close to what is really fundamental in man's emotional make-up? *Does open acknowledgement of a powerful force mean that man can no longer control that force?* Is this the unreasonable fear that separates man from full encounter with full energy?

Just as we have seen different levels of awareness and utilization of the potential of ambition, conditioned by upbringing, environment, and relationships, so there is a level of recognition of sex for every identity, conditioned by many of the same sociological dimensions. Man *had* been conditioned to keep sex a private matter. *Now* times have changed dramatically, and each identity must determine its own level against what's expected by others before it can use the energy—or at least be comfortable with it. —This chapter shows sex energies in horoscopes in relation to modern times of freer expression.

V.E. Robson's book *Astrology and Human Sex Life* deals with the subject of sex and marriage superbly. The case studies are of famous people for the most part (historically famous) and the manifestations of sex are primarily physical. Indeed, the physical act of sex is the most personally expressive and creative, and Robson's study of this side of Tchaikovsky and Oscar Wilde can reward one with a deeper understanding of these artists' works: *Eugene Onegin* and Wilde's play "Salome," for example. To free sexual energy *throughout* the identity is a modern goal, a socially valued modern embellishment, the glow that can be born within a passive personality, the self-confidence that can make a businessman more effective, the *raison d'etre* of an artistic creation. Sex in modern times is delicately but powerfully linked to self-esteem and motivation. In current case studies of people not famous, we can see how this energy in the specific is assimilated toward fulfillment in the whole.

Again, with Robson, we encounter the "higher octave" reference to planetary manifestations: "In their loftiest aspect, Uranus and Neptune, and no doubt Pluto as well, confer a very high degree of spiritual and occult development, but, unfortunately, the mass of humanity is as yet entirely incapable of responding to the intense spiritual forces that use these planets as their channel. The result, in the majority of cases, is that the force has to expend itself on emotional rather than spiritual levels. Its intensity then throws into prominence all the dormant and subconscious emotional desires, giving rise to uncontrollable excesses and magnifying what would normally be only slight emotional irregularities into overmastering perversions. . . . We must look to artistic, religious and social circles for the overwhelming majority of cases."

But modern times provide modern outlets. Social sanction for the erotic, for the creative, for the individual *does* give an opportunity for response. The subconscious emotions see the light of day, and new art forms, speech freedoms, religious concepts, dress styles, pleasure emphasis, etc., provide forms for reflection. The "common" man shares the same energies with the famous. In subjective reaction and overall sex potential they are equal. The higher octave is out in the open—at least part of it—and the identity is freed for fuller expression.

The planets have many meanings. In Horary Astrology especially, knowing the myriad rulerships is essential. If we are studying a businessman's horoscope, basically we look for the ambition and characterological factors connected with it, in relation to the client's question. As soon as we begin to talk about sex—emotional response, creativity, sociality—we must look at the planets' additional meanings, and the House system must take on a specific refinement and focus.

Venus, for example, means money, personal resources. It also stands for the social antennae, marriage harmony, affections. As Venus develops relationships with Mars, the focus can become more specifically sexual. The Mars energies gain a receptor and—much as an aggressive leader can shift an advancing army or a commercial can change opinion—invigorate other dimensions of Venus' meaning. Similarly, Saturn's structure, ambition, and classical "coldness" have an effect upon the sensitive receptor. Time influences the emotional responses enormously.

Jupiter is the "greater fortune." It expands the feelings and opinions to a larger scale, a broader application, perhaps a higher level. At the same time, Jupiter can expand negative feelings and flatten enthusiasms.

The planet Uranus has the meaning of individuation, potential eccentricity. Uranus intensifies the self, brings the unique dimension to an identity's creative statement. In relationship with Venus, Uranus can make emotional response unusual, out of the ordinary. If Mercury is involved, the mental involvement with the emotions is energized, comfortably or uncomfortably. The whole synthesis potential of a horoscope can find exclusive domain in delineating creative energy, sex.

Neptune, with its meanings of camouflage, substitution, deception, takes on more specific significance sexually: fantasy, preoccupation, often suppression of the self. Pluto seems to refer directly to the classical legend of the god of the underworld. In relation to sex, to creative energy, Pluto brings subtle attention to the underworld of emotions or to emotions in the underworld, literally. And, of course, *the public lure* of Pluto can never be forgotten (see especially the example on page 153 later in this chapter).

The Sun is always the life energy symbol and the Moon always gives personality form to this energy. The Ascendant is the thrust of the personality and the lens through which creative energy hopes to project itself.

Within five seconds, an astrologer can count the degrees between the Sun and Venus and, if the number refers to an age when marriage or sex or creative expression is reasonably possible (at a year for a degree), be on the way to understanding an identity's management of a particular sexual opportunity. Progressing the Sun to a sextile, square, or trine applies as well. (The reliability of the deduction seems unaffected by whether the Sun approaches the rapport with Venus dexterly, from behind Venus, rather than sinisterly to a Venus behihd the Sun in the birth chart.)

In the example on page104, the native has Venus in the Xth at 25 Aquarius 04 and the Sun in the XIth (ahead of Venus) at 22 Pisces 51. There are about twenty-seven degrees between them. Was he married at twenty-seven? Yes. Here the Sun goes to Venus by axial rotation, clockwise motion, or Venus comes to the Sun by the generalized degree-for-a-year formula.

The wife of the man discussed in the above example has the Sun at 19 Virgo 32 in the XIIth (page 122). Venus is in 9 Libra 58, ahead of the Sun and almost conjunct the Ascendant, rising in the XIIth. The rapport here is twenty degrees. Was she married at twenty? No, but she was engaged to be married, and the engagement was abandoned (XIIth House restrictions? Neptune, only three degrees behind the Sun, opposed by Saturn, is also in Virgo and the XIIth). —Classically, in a woman's chart, Mars identifies the male force in her socio-sexual life. We look to her Mars at 21 Leo 09 in the XIth House of hopes and wishes, love received (fifth of VIIth). Mars here rules her VIIth (marriage) and is in her "heart" (Leo). The rapport between Mars and Sun is twenty-eight degrees. She was twenty seven and a half when married.

The advertising executive-turned-artist, discussed on page 27, has Venus in 16 Aries 55, behind the IInd House Sun at 4 Taurus 53. The rapport is eighteen degrees. The year would have been 1946, during a post-war period, when people did get married quickly and early. But the powerful bucket-handle Saturn there in the Xth trines this Venus. Might ambition have been focused clearly enough to have strategically delayed marriage? But surely, this native's aesthetic sense was deeply awakened—his painting?—and very, very possibly he experienced an intense affair involving all his personal resources (IInd House). Did he have such an affair, significant to this day? Yes.

The woman whose horoscope appears on page 123 has

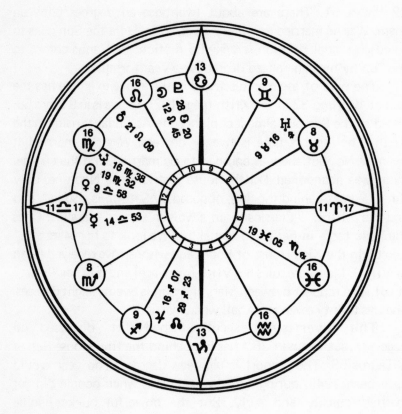

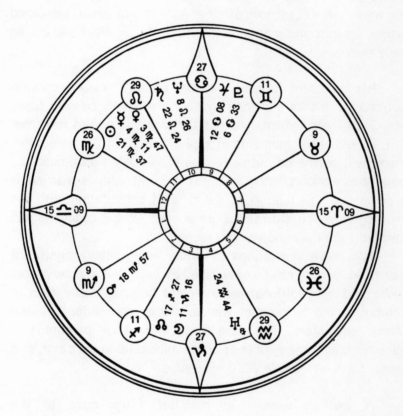

Venus in 3 Virgo 47, eighteen degrees behind the Sun, also in Virgo, in the XIth House. Would a love-hope be checked somehow by the Virgo nature and the Sun's position near the cusp of the XIIth? Mercury is in conjunction with this Venus; would good critical thinking snuff out this energy? The native did have a significant love affair at eighteen, as well as awakened artistic interest and school study in art. Practicality ruled out an early marriage.

It's important to note that such rapport measurements do not *cause* romance and marriage, art awakening, creative flow, sex. Such measurements are not the *sine qua non* of romance. But, should these moments of rapport occur in the horoscope, there will surely be something with which an astrologer can begin his work covering sex. —If a client who is married is experiencing this rapport at the time of consultation with the astrologer, sex considerations are a most reliable beginning and invariably are the reason help is sought.

Two more illustrations can show how a vitally significant key to an identity can be established by swift, initial observation. —We add an additional measurement here, so easily seen in computing the horoscope: the parallel of declination between Venus and Mars. The parallel is a kind of psychological alinement, as if the symbol of one is placed upon the other, as if Venus takes on a subtle yet driving edge.

A married woman in her late fifties came to this astrologer to ask about a businessman in his late forties. The man lived some distance away. She said simply that he was troubled in his employment and personal life. The woman calmly added that she and this man had been having a covert liaison for several years. He had been divorced some years before. His chart (p.125) disclosed a Scorpio Ascendant, with Mars in Aries in the Vth. The Moon was in Taurus in the VIIth, squaring

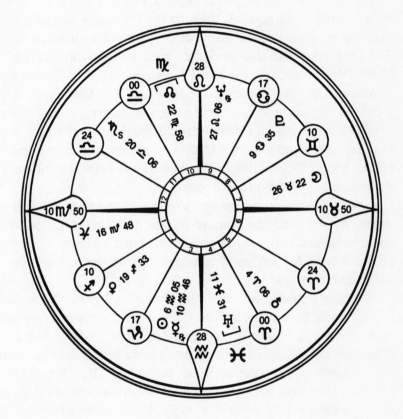

Neptune conjunct the Leo Midheaven. Saturn was stationary in Libra in the XIth (his ambition needed love; was the balance good?). Venus was in 19 Sagittarius in the IInd, forty-seven degrees behind the Sun in Aquarius in the IIIrd. He was forty-seven years old at that time, and Venus, Mars, and Jupiter were in progressed parallel. Viewing the horoscope sexually, the man would have been experiencing intense sexual expression. The progressed Sun was very near to a sextile with the public Moon (Moon opposing the rising Jupiter in Scorpio). Jupiter and Neptune rule this Pisces position near the Vth cusp. The inquiring woman was calm and objective, interested in helping him. She simply didn't seem actively involved in the problem. Because he had no wife, the Moon perhaps referred to this man's public image, "camouflaged" tensely by the Neptune square in the House of profession and honor.

With the rapport between Venus and the Sun, reinforced deeply by the parallels, overseen by ambition's need for love and acceptance, the native quite possibly had had his cover lifted, his affairs *within his job* perhaps exposed. This *was* the problem: bureaucratic scandal.

In the example on page 64, we see a Scorpio Ascendant and a Cancer Sun in the VIIIth. There was no immediate rapport measurement. One with Venus *would* occur at age forty-five and, after full analysis, this proved to be a key to future developments and present hopes (Venus ruled the XIth). But the parallel between Mars and Venus occurred at seventeen and the transits of Mars-Saturn conjoined the radix Mars, ruler of the Vth, positioned in Libra in the XIth. Might something have happened to this very emotionally oriented woman? At such an early age, was there a *rude* (Saturn-Mars transit of radix Mars) sexual awakening? Yes, there was: she was raped.

The quick approximation of rapport between Sun and Venus or Mars and an acknowledgement of Mars-Venus parallels start the process of analysis moving into the department of creativity, emotions and their absorption or deployment. A dialogue between astrologer and client begins. Other factors are discovered, and the significance of sex within the horoscope begins to define itself.

The House Axes

The Houses also can take on specifically sexual meanings, slight ramifications of classical meanings with a sexual focus. The Vth House is probably the most important in the initial consideration of sex: love, creativity, children, pleasures, drama. The opposite House, the XIth, is the partner's Vth, the partner's love, creativity, pleasures, etc. The XIth signifies the hopes and wishes of the native and, in terms of sex, the love hoped for, the love received. Much of sex expression involves relationships, of course; we must be aware of the House axes, the give-and-take with sexual energy.

I-VII

This axis suggests the egos involved. The first is the native's personality thrust; the seventh is the kind of person he attracts. Here are areas that can disclose the protagonists in sexual drama: a marriage, an artistic partnership, a public projection.

II-VIII

This axis involves resources. The second House is too easily thought of as only "money." In studying sex, the second House can represent the embodiment (the personal value) of the entire creative spirit as in the example on page 26. In a very real and modern sense, the second House can become the actual self, if the identity is on public display, offering himself at a price. Public performers have a very sensitive second House: they are commodities.

Additionally, the second can mean just plain money connected with sex. The example on page 128 shows Venus in

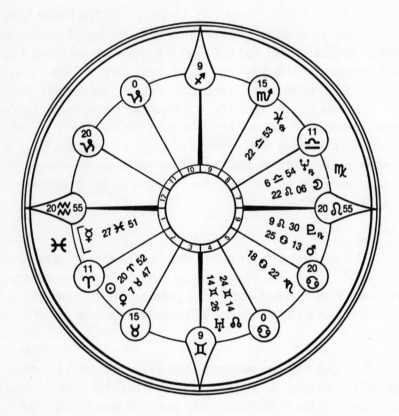

Taurus in the IInd squaring Pluto in Leo in the VIth. This handsome, athletic man with an Aries Sun also in the IInd *preferred* sex with prostitutes. He needed to pay for physical pleasure. When the Sun progressed to a conjunction with Venus and entered the square to Pluto at seventeen years, he was actually arrested at a bawdy party. Pluto and the underworld! Of course, there are other factors in this horoscope that supply a possible motivation for this preference.

The VIIIth is the partner's resources. They may be opposed in nature to those indicated by the native's IInd. The example in the preceding paragraph has a retrograde Jupiter in the VIIIth opposing his IInd House Sun. Mars is in square with the Sun from the VIth. —The native suffers from premature orgasm (Mars in Cancer square Aries Sun in II). Mars calls forth his personal resources quickly, passionately. His partners' (Jupiter retrograde in Libra) "resources" seek an expansion of his attentions and enthusiasms to accommodate their resources and values, and, because of his underachievement, leave him. Prostitutes don't complain.

III-IX

Here is where we see both parties' *mental* reactions to sex: to marriage, culture, paintings, concerts, anything emotional, expressive. Additionally, we should read this House for travel, honeymoons, separations by distance.

The case described on page 36 can be amplified by viewing her horoscope on page 130. With Jupiter and Saturn in the IIIrd, their midpoint squared by a VIIth House Cancer Moon presents two different sides of the native's sex life to the public. She is expansive about a positive front, thinking this is important to her image, and openly critical about sex energy to her husband. The result is enormous tension and great frustration. Her IInd House Sun opposes an VIIIth House Neptune (his IInd): she expects something from him that he isn't; her own resources

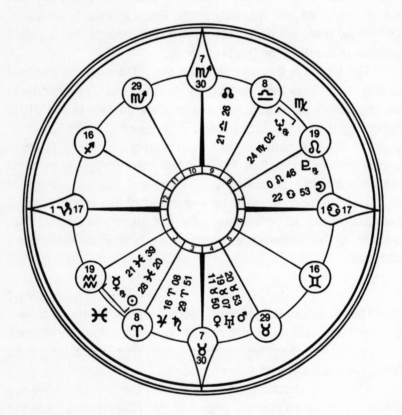

are fantasized (Sun-Neptune opposition). Her favorable IXth gives her respite from tension when he travels (his IIIrd).

IV-X

This axis involves in-laws and the inhibitions therefrom; also the cause of the end, as well as impotency. For example: a woman divorced her husband when the Sun progressed to square the XIth House Uranus. Would Neptune in the IVth, opposed by Saturn in the Xth, simply mean that the husband was different than he seemed; had his ambition for the marriage and his work gone to sleep? —A simple observation like this often releases a stream of response from a client, and the result is what Astrology should be: a dynamic dialogue, a sharing of identity. In this illustration, Neptune ruled her XIth, hopes and wishes, love received.

I have no example for the impotency factor. But impotency is directly related to self-esteem, job honor (the native's Xth, the spouse's IVth and vice versa). Preoccupation with or feelings of failure are directly linked to emotional depression. We should look to the IVth-Xth axis for corroboration.

V-XI

Here is perhaps the most important axis for first consideration. Mars or Uranus here certainly should suggest that we look for ardor and/or eccentricity in the creative functions. Mars or Venus *retrograde* here in a woman's horoscope can often mean no success or considerable difficulty with orgasm. There is a kind of energy and/or emotional counterpoint working, an expectation or dream unfulfilled. Orgasm for a woman is figuratively a release of love. Modern fiction and love manuals stress orgasm's importance, and the female with difficulty here loses self-esteem with respect to what she thinks society and her partner expect of her. Saturn present here in the Vth in a woman's horoscope often seems to indicate an overly structured

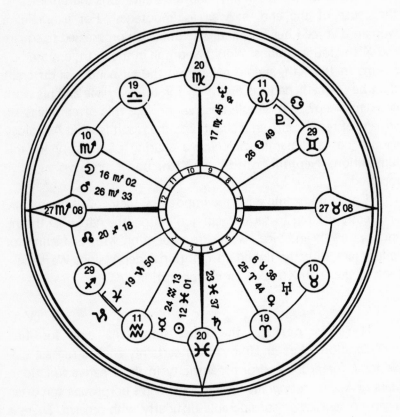

sexual ambition, a portioning out of physical sex "service" to her husband. And, often, difficulty with orgasm is coincidental.

In relation to the Vth House, we should discuss Venus in Aries, anywhere in the horoscope, especially for a female, particularly if it is posited in V: Venus in Aries is a tease, a symbol of sex often without the substance. Marilyn Monroe as a motion-picture sex-symbol personified this teasing, provocative-unattainable-ideal of Venus in Aries. Aries is too "fast," too "hot" for Venus. Venus takes on Amazonian proportions, says Evangeline Adams, but lacks follow-through. Venus as ruler of Taurus and Libra needs anchor, rest, balance, and flattery.

The woman whose horoscope appears on page 132, has a Scorpio Ascendant, Mars rising in the XIIth House, Venus in Aries in the Vth, with Uranus there in Taurus. The woman worked overtime at being provocative. But, with the Moon in Scorpio in the XIIth and the Sun in Pisces in the IIIrd opposing Neptune in the IXth, the personality was preoccupied with sex, with emotional fantasies involving mental expectancy of sex (Venus rules the XIth). The native just couldn't follow through in a real sexual situation. She became an accountant with a musical organization (a sexual-aesthetic substitution) and was unable to achieve orgasm; in fact, she knew little to nothing about her own physical potentials and anatomy. She was extremely nervous in her concern.

The example on page 102, with Saturn in the XIth opposing Neptune in the Vth, where the need for social acceptance fights with the ambition to follow a lifetime dream of artistic endeavor, reveals a subtle sex dimension as well. The native remarked to this astrologer that the sex life had tapered off "normally" (mid-thirties!). Ambition *throughout the sex spectrum* had fallen asleep! The need for personal endorsement had been projected onto society, and the arena of XIth House ambition had substituted for personal giving and receiving.

Uncannily, at this very moment, writing this page, this astrologer now in Germany received a call from new clients in Paris. The husband and wife needed help. Birth information was given and a

Wife

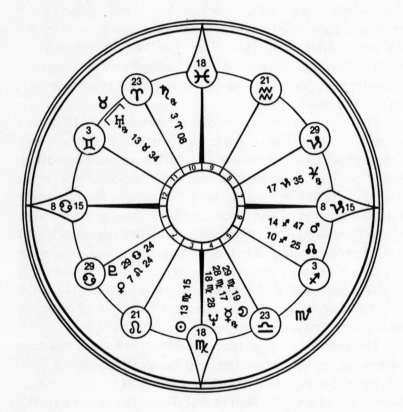

return call arranged. No indication of the concern was offered. This writing was interrupted, and the horoscopes were drawn. They presented a most appropriate example of sexual consideration involving most of the variables above.

In the wife's horoscope, page 134, only Jupiter, Uranus, and Saturn are above the horizon—all retrograde: something might be holding the woman down or pressing her into herself. The Xth House Saturn retrograde is in Aries: determined ambition, plus some counterpoint—perhaps inferiority feelings because of early homelife or early ambitions unfulfilled—and open self-defensiveness. Moon in Virgo opposes Saturn from IV, the home; Moon ruling the Cancer Ascendant. Sun and Neptune conjoined in Virgo frame the IVth cusp; Mercury retrograde is conjunct the IVth House Moon, also in Virgo. —Here was the mental and hypercritical nature, concentrating her defenses in the home.

The Vth House has Libra on the cusp with Scorpio intercepted. Venus is in Leo (affections, drama) in the IInd, with Pluto, and Mars is in Sagittarius in the VIth, in trine to Venus.

What is the sexual profile? The Mars-Venus trine would indicate that the wife's sexuality flowed well. But Mars is squared by her Sun, suggesting a tense energy edge to the Virgo personality and, sexually, perhaps a clash with the husband about her sexual fulfillment. Her VIIIth (his IInd) is ruled by the Saturn retrograde in X, opposed by her Virgo Moon: could it be that his resources didn't match her needs, her mental judgment of what she should expect? The love received by her: her XIth (his Vth) has Aries on the cusp with Taurus intercepted, involving again the Mars-Venus rulerships. Uranus is there, indicating perhaps something sudden, unusual, unique about these matters. Additionally, the rapport between Venus and Sun corresponds with the call to the astrologer.

The husband's horoscope has a Scorpio Sun in the VIIIth, widely conjunct a Sagittarian Mercury. The Saturn is retrograde in Pisces, intercepted in the XIIth, opposing the Virgo Neptune intercepted in the VIth. Here, the man's efforts to distill his

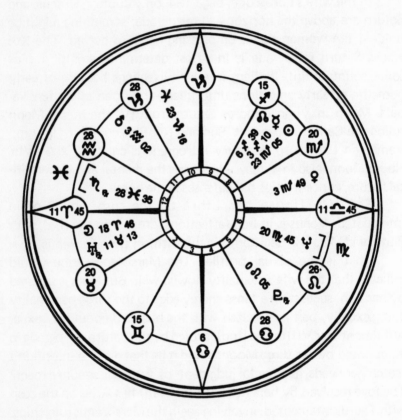

ambition would cause restriction, perhaps an emotional difficulty accepting the leadership he needs and facing up to situations. His Vth House has Pluto in Leo, opposed by Mars in the XIth: something "undercover . . . . or covered under" about sex; and the Mars again pointing out his partner's ardor. This Mars-Pluto opposition was squared by the Scorpio Venus in the VIIth! Sex, giving, loving had difficulty and tension (Venus rules the Libra VIIth and the Taurus IInd) involving the wife and homelife.

His IVth and Vth Houses have Cancer cusps. The Moon was rising in the Ist just below the *Aries* Ascendant. The Moon, his personality's form, the ruler of his sex, pleasure, children, love, etc., and his home, was in Aries, and so energized, *but it was in no major aspect within the horoscope* (the approaching square to Jupiter was developing): the personality's form was pushed and wandered "out of control" with regard to sex matters. Might the problem be premature ejaculation? It was. But the syndrome spread itself throughout the personality's expressiveness, especially with regard to the veiled VIIth House Sun energy.

Of course, the reading of these symbols in this husband-wife example is presented *only* to clarify the sexual dimension. The wife's critical expectancies were doing nothing to stabilize, economize his ardor—or his presentation of self to the public in other dimensions. Yet her mental faculties could be redirected to work positively toward improving the situation, as well as to make them both open to changes of approach and expectation.

The horoscopes spoke eloquently *about other things.* The husband and wife are talented people and very successful. They face major job and home shifts—another level of self-esteem and home tension—and the one situation casts a glare upon the "other" situation. Freeing the sexual tension could enable their self-confidence and creative energies to make the best shift in the business and home dimensions.

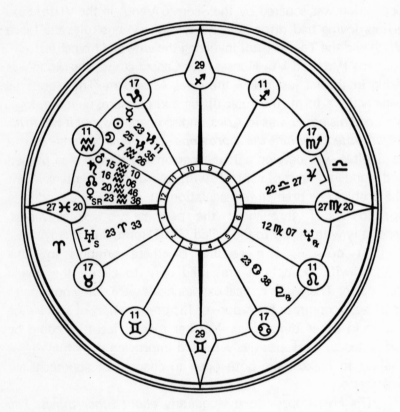

VI-XII

We have just seen in the husband's horoscope how restrictions arising from personal insecurities about performance corresponded to the Saturn-opposed-Neptune XII-VI axis.

The example on page 138 depicts a Saturn-Mars-Venus retrograde conjunction in the XIIth in Aquarius. The Sun rules the VIth (second of the Vth, partners' XIIth: her valuation of her sexuality and her partners' supposedly "camouflaged" failings). The Sun and Mercury are in conjunction in the XIth in Capricorn, opposing a Cancer Pluto in the Vth. There could well be some emotional counterpoint at work here (Venus retrograde in the XIIth, in the large conjunction). Her partners would think marvelously about her and give her respect and dignity (XIth, love received, Mercury ruling the VIIth, Libra intercepted there) but remain a little at a distance, maybe bewildered by her expectations. The Moon ruling the Vth makes no real, clear aspect and is in the XIth, neither with the Sun-Mercury nor with the XIIth House group.

The woman wandered from partner to partner seeking some emotional dream. There was *no* difficulty with orgasm but there was an emotional unfulfillment (Venus retrograde). Her personal restriction was complex and in adult life was intensified by hospital confinement and breast amputation due to the disease cancer. The confinement was definitely delineated in the horoscope (not in our discussion here) and was the core of the native's "counterpoint" and wandering.

In the study of the sexual dimensions of the horoscope, the Moon takes on very special meaning as ruler of emotional and home-life Cancer. The sister of the example discussed above has the Moon in Capricorn in the Vth. The Sun is in Leo in the XIth squaring Uranus in the IXth. Pluto and Mars are in Cancer in conjunction, also in the XIth. The native has some very obscure and anxious expectations about her love relationship. Saturn retrograde in Pisces in the VIIth, opposing a rising Neptune on the Virgo Ascendant, suggests real fantasy and camouflage in her marriage, especially since a retrograde Sagittarian Jupiter squares this opposition axis from the IVth, the home, the partner's honor (his Xth). This Capricorn Moon is classically demanding, emotionally authoritative, and "ruthless" in some cases. Here, the native used sex as a weapon against her husband, to control him—mainly because of her inferiority feelings about interrupted education and an incomplete image presented to others (crucial for a Leo). —The Moon was trine to the elevated Uranus in the IXth: she got away with it!

When the Moon is in the XIIth, the emotional personality—the personality in the form indicated by the Sign—is hidden away. Invariably, this suggests very private sexual considerations: a famous cultural leader has a XIIth House Moon in Gemini. This client has Virgo on the Vth with Libra intercepted. Mercury (also ruling the Gemini Ascendant), Venus, and Uranus are in triple conjunction at the Midheaven with the Mars-Sun conjunction, also in the Xth, all in Aquarius. The Moon squares Sun-Mars and trines Mercury-Uranus. (When Saturn and then Uranus came to this sensitive Moon during World War II, he was imprisoned.) The solitude of the personality and the constantly present private depth gain occasional external form: he published a book of poetry about love and the kiss, which would embarrass his image much; and he even used his real name (links to the Xth, honor and demand for recognition). His bureaucratic aloofness prohibits anyone from daring to mention this private sexual-aesthetic expression!

I have another case where the woman's hidden emotional hope was to have a baby with a lover in a foreign country, without marriage, away from her homeland where she is a public figure. Such situations are reported in newspapers (movie stars; even Britain's youngest member of Parliament, Bernadette

Devlin), and there is little social stigma. They are modern outlets for an eternal need. The woman of this case has the Sun in Cancer and the Moon in Leo in the XIIth House.

Abortion, the pill, promiscuity. All these are in our modern life, on our minds, in our news. The sexual dimensions of an identity have modern lures, modern modes, modern expectations, modern problems, modern pleasures. The Sign that appears on the cusp of the Vth can be a good guide, directing us to a measurement of the native's particular "stand" regarding his sexual identity:

Aries on the Vth:	an energetic thrust; rash speculation about outlets
Taurus on the Vth:	earthy, faithful, more solid and mono-dimensional
Gemini on the Vth:	duality or multiplicity; love letters
Cancer on the Vth:	deeply feeling, impressionable; home, children important
Leo on the Vth:	love as a "lever" or as final fulfillment; drama
Virgo on the Vth:	mental love, over-analysis, critical tendencies
Libra on the Vth:	socially oriented love, ego reflection; potential refinement
Scorpio on the Vth:	secrecy, depths; much control or none at all
Sagittarius on the Vth:	ideals; hunt more important than catch; expansiveness
Capricorn on the Vth:	sex is sex; maybe ambitious motive
Aquarius on the Vth:	usually other than average; innovative

Pisces on the Vth: absorbing; receptive; expecting
much

The gender of the Sign can be a sophisticated source of corroboration of other deductions. Aries, Gemini, Leo, Libra, Sagittarius, and Aquarius (the odd-numbered Signs) are masculine. The others are feminine. One female client, one of the few females in her profession, has every planet, the Ascendant and Midheaven in masculine Signs. Only her Sun in Pisces is in a feminine Sign, in the Vth. She is quite feminine appearing, but her job and mode of expression are definitely masculine. She can be a tough "cookie," doing a man's job well. There is absolutely no reason from this alinement to suspect lesbianism That would be a gross generality and a false deduction. But we can say, "When you were young, everyone probably told you you should have been a boy!" This brings humor and rapport. The native had come to grips with her expressions and motivations. She even had a feminized masculine first name! This remark got to a core of concern in a flash.

An emphasis on feminine Signs in a male's horoscope suggests increased sensitivity and emotional judgments. Note the example on page 103.

Homosexuality

Homosexuality is a sexual form of homosociality. Socially, the identity seeks a mirror image of his own particular emotional and creative energy profile. *Heterosexuals relate more for complement; homosexuals, for reinforcement.* Homosexuality is an expansion of ego-definition (or destruction), basically narcissistic in origin and reward. We are not concerned here with the supposed causes, psychodynamically, of homosexuality. (Psychological research and texts related to this subject should certainly be in every astrologer's library.) We are concerned with finding this dimension in a horoscope in order to see identity completely and to be most helpful. Today, when homosexuality is open and when bisexuality is definitely a mode of expression for many, this alinement of value and energies is very important. To overlook, demean or hush it up, dams energy flow and diminishes identity.

If the long-held stigma about homosexuality is removed, identities can be more fully expressive without guilt and constriction. The social discomfort many people feel about homosexuality is not an expression of a universal or instinctive taboo. Many cultures in diverse lands and times accommodated homosexuality easily and practically, with honor. Cultural needs in terms of organization, growth, and cooperation are reflected in the value systems related to the expression of sex: certain art forms or styles can easily shock a society as much as the revelation of an unusual sexual preference. The word "scandal" is used for a music event, a painting, a play, a sculpture, a political statement, a book, as well as for an act or style of physical sex expression, whether or not the non-physical forms have anything whatever to do with biology or anatomy. A miscarriage of justice, a travesty, can be "scandalous" because *it goes against what is expected by most people or by a cultural code.* But today, with the cultural accent on diversity, individuality, invention, experimentation, and "doing your own thing," going against what is expected is a necessary means to an indivudual and collective end. Change and diversity—of attitudes and expression—are essential to growth.

The individual identity finds itself with personal needs for expression, often fantasized to an extreme, in a society that often prescribes other means and goals. The tension that results vitalizes identity-change. *Management of this tension governs the quality of development, the level of growth, the fulfillment of the identity.*

In the horoscope on page 144 one sees all the bodies in the eastern half of the horoscope, accenting the ego portion of the

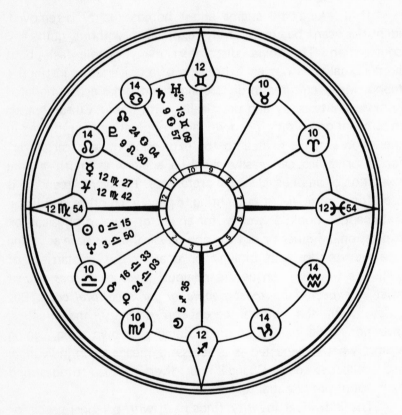

identity. There is no opposition (Moon approaching Uranus), suggesting a difficulty finding external focus, and the angles have mutable Signs—a further corroboration. The polarities of the House and Sign axes are incomplete in "face-to-face" fashion, though, of course, they can be established by planetary rulerships. The Virgo Ascendant has its ruler Mercury in exact conjunction with Jupiter on the horizon. The Libra Sun is in the Ist, suggesting enormous ego-awareness and definition.

An important note: we have seen that Virgo on the Vth may indicate love upon the mental plane, over-analysis, critical tendencies. This capsule-key includes the tendency to *rationalization*, especially when the ego is so emphasized. But wherever Virgo is, there is this mental *fastidiousness* and, with homosexuality, this factor becomes very significant. Classic meanings of Virgo—that it indicates a delayed marriage because one waits too long for the ideal, and opportunities pass by—can change subtly in a modern situation. Virgo can mean finding this ideal *in one's self or in one very like one's self.* The fastidious nature, the hypercritical fussiness, the preoccupation with cleanliness and detail can be projected *against* established norms and introduce the structure of an esoteric group or fraternity. All subgroupings in society seek to define themselves through ritual, costume, behavior, qualifications. The homosexual, through Virgo, embodies often the rationalization and highly mental arrangement of his own ideal.

Here, the Virgo Ascendant, accentuated so by the Mercury-Jupiter conjunction, suggests a very developed critical, fussy, "exclusive" rationale about ego projection (squared by the Moon).

Uranus is the planet of self-accentuation. Its manifestations can range from deciding to move from one city or job to another to discovering a "new" star. The identity is emphasized, the self is accentuated. (Astronomers and other scientists reward their discoveries by attaching their own names to them!) Uranus is the planet of self-discovery as well as of objective invention, of genius. It is powerfully linked to the individualistic use of sexual energy. Notice how, with established geniuses in history, there seem to be "eccentric" personality traits, as well as highly individualized sex expression.

In this horoscope, Uranus is conjunct the Midheaven, in Mercury's Sign and square to the Ascendant and the Mercury-Jupiter conjunction. The self is uniquely intensified, the mind and critical abilities (defenses?) are under sharp tension. Uranus rules half of the Vth and is in the Xth: sex, the profession, and individual honor are involved. Saturn is in the Xth also, in Cancer: determination, yes, but a deep need for encouragement, perhaps not received in early homelife. Saturn rules the Vth and is the only planet in a Water Sign, Cancer. The home, emotions, the ambition, the profession, encouragement (especially to one with mutable Signs on all Angles—suggesting a reactant personality) are all in powerful focus.

The Sun is in conjunction with Neptune in Libra. Here is fantasy and camouflage, in the Ist in Venus' Sign, more corroboration. The Sun rules the XIIth House of personal restrictions. The ego shields itself against restrictions through fantasy.

Venus is in wide conjunction with Mars in Libra in the IInd and in wide trine to Uranus. With so much Mercury emphasis (Ascendant, Uranus in Gemini, Midheaven, the square and the trine); with Neptune—music, art, theatrical illusion—conjunct the Sun in Venus' Libra, Neptune ruling the public VIIth, Pisces, and the co-ruler Jupiter, with Mercury on the Ascendant—with this Mercury and Neptune emphasis, might the native be a public-performer, an artist? Does his professional ambition call for encouragement in an aesthetic profession? Yes. He is a singer seeking international outlets (Venus rules the IXth).

The Moon is in Sagittarius (ruled by Jupiter on the Ascendant with Mercury) and is in the IIIrd (communications, travel, mental faculties; the eleventh of the Vth, the hopes and dreams for his sexual energy, his creative expression). The Moon trines Pluto in Leo (drama, loves) in the XIth—further corroboration. The Moon is approaching an awareness-opposition to Uranus. Additionally, Venus parallels Jupiter, Saturn parallels Uranus, the Sun parallels Neptune.

The ego emphasis, the physical and mental fastidiousness and rationalization associated with Mercury, tension over ambition, the need for acclaim, personal values seeking unique recognition, the camouflage—these are the characteristics of a homosexual. The native *is* a homosexual and, in this day and age, is "comfortable" being one. He doesn't feel that it is a problem. He is successful in this expression (Moon sextile Sun-Neptune).

But the problem does become one of drawing acclaim to ambition for job proficiency. *Sex success took the place of actual job achievement.* Success with others like himself in his own field was becoming the higher priority. To give Saturn its due freedom, the call here was to separate sex from the job-situation.

In the horoscope on page 148, again the Sun is in conjunction with Neptune, exact conjunction, in Virgo on the Vth, with Mars as well, Libra intercepted. Here again we can expect the camouflage, the fantasy somehow in the life energy. The Virgo dimension here echoes the Ascendant in Gemini, both ruled by Mercury, which is also in the Vth in Libra.

Saturn is rising, stationary in the XIIth House in wide conjunction with intensifying, individualistic Uranus, both in Gemini, squared by the Moon in emotional Pisces in the professional Xth. The man's ambition is highly adaptable, vacillating between the conventional and the idiosyncratic, with keen perceptions en route to fulfillment. We could expect this to be uniquely alined through Uranus. With the square from the "public" Moon in the professional Xth, we could expect that he would make a profession out of some part of his perceptive and

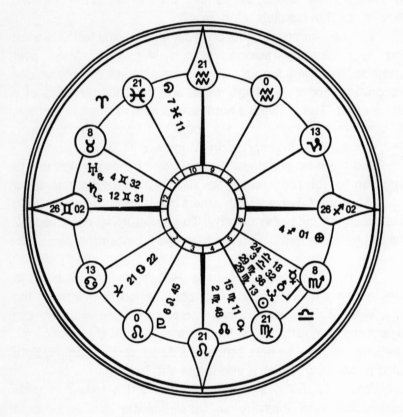

highly critical fantasy-creativity (Saturn-Uranus are also wide trine—across the Sign line—to the Neptune-Sun-Mars conjunction in the Vth; additionally, Venus squares Saturn).

The Moon square Saturn and/or Uranus is always very important. This is the aspect that is correlated with advance. This correlation holds for Sun square Saturn too, and for Moon and/or Sun conjunctions or oppositions with Mars or Saturn. In these aspects, ambition and energy-drive invigorate the personality's form and/or the life energy. The presidents of the United States always seem to share one or more of these configurations. I call this Moon-square-Saturn, in particular, *the expansion aspect,* contrary to the classic constriction meanings for Saturn. This aspect *signifies tension between the personality's form and ambition's call,* a tension which brings development. In progressions, whenever this expansion aspect occurs, so can development.

In this horoscope example, the progressed Moon would be opposite its own position in thirteen years or so, nearing the radix Venus and squaring again the radix Saturn-Uranus. At the same time, Saturn would be opposite its own place, about to enter the VIIth, a public showing. The rapport measurement here between Venus and Sun-Neptune is also fourteen degrees. What happened then? The native decided that he was exclusively homosexual.

Venus in Virgo widely opposes the Moon and widely squares Saturn-Uranus. As ruler of Libra, intercepted in the Vth and of the XIIth where Saturn-Uranus are, Venus is very involved here; also, Venus would be exalted in the Moon's Sign Pisces.

Jupiter is in square with the Libra Mercury from the IInd House and in wide trine with the Moon. As with every Full-Moon birth, the Part of Fortune is always near the Descendant, here in the VIth (work, service), opposing Saturn-Uranus, etc. Might this native have taken his sexuality and, driven by the power and expansion factors and *his keen observations of ambition's way,* channelled it into a profession, to public profit? Yes. He first became an interior decorator (Venus in IV, home, sextile Jupiter in II in Cancer), but when Saturn returned to its birth position, a new way was chosen to express the whole configuration. He left his interior decorating field when ambition conflicted with his fantasized life energy (Saturn transit opposed Sun-Neptune from the XIth) and, with a partner (Jupiter, ruler of VIII in the IInd), opened several elegant pornography stores in a major European city, just as Saturn zeroed in on its birth position. There was friction with the partner (Jupiter square Mercury), who chose to stay out of the picture at home (Jupiter in Cancer). By Saturn's complete return to its birth position, the stores were under way, excellently managed, and very successful.

Masturbation

Masturbation etymologically refers to "stirring up, to disturbing," from the Italo-Latin roots. Onanism is a classical Biblical reference to the "sin" of Onan, i.e., the spilling of his seed upon the ground. (Onanism didn't seem to apply to women!) The German language pays homage to Onan with *onanieren* and *Onanie,* but also adds *Selbstbefriedigung,* self-enjoyment. Our English, reflecting our Puritan beginnings, concocts *self-abuse, self-pollution.* Masturbation can definitely cause the biological phenomenon of orgasm (in men, the spilling of the seed). *It is also a reaction, a response to bio-neurological pressure.* The monkeys at the zoo masturbate at any given moment, not to abuse themselves, not to pollute themselves, but perhaps to relieve bioneurological pressure built up in their metabolism or through their social position and strivings within the group. Tense horses waiting to perform at a circus have emissions to relieve their nervousness.

Because masturbation is so linked to the nervous system, in fact, in the male, to the whole procreation system, *it is an extremely important link with and reinforcement of identity.* It is a so-called adolescent phenomenon not just because the glands are ready, but because the identity is in need of confimation, reinforcement. I am a man! An enormous oversight is that masturbation is so easily thought of as a male activity. This is because the male produces an ejaculation, Onan's seed. Of course, the phenomenon of orgasm is shared by both sexes; easier for some than for others, due to anatomy, nervous system, and psycho-social pressure. At adolescence, wih the onset of menstruation, the female becomes aware of her ability to have children; the sensations of and attention to her genitalia become more focused and meaningful. New tensions and feelings arise.

An orgasm produced during sleep, produced by the body's system, the mind in dream, or by external stimuli in the environment (a rocking train car, for example), is a system's reaction. With orgasm, a system recognizes its potential and is fulfilled. A new preparation-time ensues, a time to approach life again. Conscious "stirring up" to orgasm in both sexes is an *effort to define identity in a moment of recognized potential.*

Young children, little babies, animals, adults all belong to this fulfillment continuum. With a mind and imagination, secondary motives are born and an aesthetic (including love) takes over to glorify the ego more often, more dramatically, more pleasurably. When *guilt* intrudes through parental, social or religious teaching, the will to fulfill this physical potential is thwarted, and problems rise.

Today, masturbation is not so hidden as it was. The word, and its synonyms, the act, the embellishments, the understanding of it all, even occasional medical sanction, are with us every day. Students under pressure in college can masturbate in order to fall asleep. The interruption of a sexual relationship, due to a partner's extended travel in modern times, can be made more bearable by relaxing sexual anxiety through masturbation. The astrologer often must deal with these considerations.

It would be hard to imagine a chart that said outright:

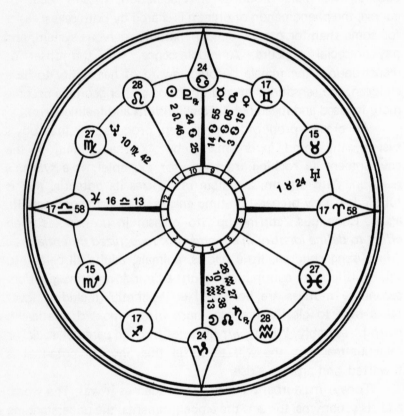

"prostitute, homosexual, thief, president, painter, management consultant." But we have discussed the modern era's recognition of the diffusion of sexual energies through a broad spectrum of creative activities. Many of these activities have *always been* sexual, but because of frank recognition the sexual energies can flow more openly and profitably. The following example is of an extremely sexual woman, well married, highly intelligent, attractive, a fine mother of several children. She and her husband explore their sexual potential together on a grand scale, centered on individual and mutual masturbation. For this woman, the energy flows splendidly. Without her ease of expression it could be ruinous.

In the horoscope on page 152, the Libra Ascendant puts Aquarius on the Vth: we would wonder about the unusual, innovative, or unique dimension of her sexual energy. Venus, ruler of the Ascendant, is in close conjunction with Mars in the IXth. Here is excitement and fiery emotional energy linked to her personality thrust and affirmation. Additionally, the woman is married to a foreigner, and they live in still another foreign country.

Uranus rules the Vth and is in the VIIth—hopefully she would have such a unique partner as well. In fact, she was married previously, her particular energies were blocked, and she married her present husband, sexually compatible with her, when Uranus transited her Ascendant and Jupiter.

Uranus is squared by both the Sun and the Moon, at this exact Full-Moon birth! Uranus is in Venus' Taurus, the Moon is in Uranus' Aquarius, and the Sun is in its own Sign Leo in the Xth! The unique personality form (Moon in Aquarius) given to the powerful emotional nature, the zenith of the native's existence (Sun in Leo in the Xth), is made individual and electrified by these squares to Uranus. (Uranus is also in sextile with Mars-Venus.) Pluto in conjunction with the Cancer Midheaven gives a kind of public lure to the powerful emotional axis (and is parallel Venus). Mercury in Cancer in the IXth is square to the rising Jupiter: Gemini and Sagittarius rule the "writing and mental" IX-III axis. This synthesis leads to the fact that she and her husband love to write about their most intimate sexual experiences, make and receive telephone calls during the sex act, make photographs and tape recordings. They masturbate while reading their own and others' letters.

Neptune in the XIth further records the unusual love received from the husband (sextiled by Mars-Venus), who perhaps suppresses his own self to accommodate her. The retrograde Saturn in Aquarius indicates an ambition projected socially for unique recognition and, in the IVth and Vth, involves the home, children, in-laws, etc. The native has taken on the children of her husband's first marriage, maintains expanded family ties with her own family and her new husband's. The early home years were difficult but do not concern us here.

Such a sexual woman reinforces her ego and competes in the world with her unique expression at many levels. (The T Cross—Sun, Moon, Uranus—is discharged into the ego Ascendant.) There are other details at the sexual level that correspond to all the aspects outlined above: the sex life is "olympic" and definitely geared to exhibitionism, but kept completely unto themselves. Fantasy and distant communications become the audience. With all the emphasis on the home axis and on the Sign Cancer, it is not surprising that the couple does not involve other partners in their activities, except as correspondents. Though they have a very extraverted cultural and community life, their sex is confined to their home and mail and phone communications with others like them.

This case shows the extent to which one can need to be sexually expressive and privately fulfilled. The family is very happy and successful; the husband is a community leader and executive. They are both polylingual.

What if these drives were not freed? Where would the

energy go? What problems would be caused by the guilt and the frustration? This case shows sex *fulfilled* in an individual extreme. In other cases, some of these drives and desires or other sexual needs may be unfulfilled and cause problems in marriage, self-esteem, communication, relationships. When the astrologer can uncover such a preoccupation or concern, he can relieve the client's anxiety about idiosyncracy and help to free the enormous energies from guilt and restriction, from hiding. *Often, the astrologer's very discovery of the sex dimension and its importance to a client takes away the fear and isolation usually felt by those with such needs! Sex is normal; identity is individual; reasonable fulfillment is freedom.* —And with experience, one learns very quickly that such a case as this, though extreme in delineation, is really not so unusual at all!

Horoscopes of the famous and historical in most cases are not rewarding in depth study of the personal sex quotient. Their private lives are rarely known except in rare instances when the sexual energy itself is the reason for fame. In many cases, the horoscopically obvious sexual profile—and *everyone* has a sexual profile!—was channeled significantly into varying forms of identity expression that afforded lasting fame.

Queen Victoria's Mars and Venus in Aries, her Mercury in Taurus, and the New Moon in Gemini with the Sun—*all in the XIIth*—certainly give us a profile of the woman whose name, whose very ego-projection, labeled an age.

Her predecessor, Henry the VIIIth had a retrograde Saturn in the Vth, in "unusual" Aquarius. The Cancer Sun in the Xth opposed the IVth House Uranus and both were squared by the public Moon in Aries in the VIIth. This is powerful, individual, eccentric ambition led by a complicated sexual drive indeed. Mars rising above the Virgo Ascendant certainly suggests cold-blooded detachment in seeing his ambition to fulfillment, even clashing with the Church (square to Jupiter in the IXth) to regulate law to fit his multiple marriages.

Lincoln had Venus in Aries, with Aries on the Vth. We don't know of his private profile, but this Venus is trine the Saturn-Neptune conjunction upon the Sagittarius Ascendant. Venus' flame is given enormous stature here, suggesting a high-minded aesthetic linked with the core of the personality's projection. An idealism was achieved and this energy went to his profession, his dreams, and his service (Venus rules parts of the Xth, the XIth, the VIth) for his homeland (Venus in IV).

The dignity and sedateness of Woodrow Wilson—Capricorn Sun in the IVth, opposing the Midheaven Saturn in Cancer, all planets in the western half of the horoscope—was dedicated to relationships with others, the world. His ambition needed deep personal reinforcement and acclaim. His unusual sex profile (Aquarius on the Vth) was certainly at the depth of this need: Mars and Venus were in conjunction in the Vth in Aquarius and squared the individualistic Uranus, ruler of the Vth, in the VIIIth. —Modern researchers with the curiosity of modern, freer times (!) uncovered his love letters and affairs, written and conducted while he was in the White House. Though president, he was still an identity seeking personal fulfillment.

Thomas Edison dealt with mysteries, striving to conquer them uniquely. He had a Scorpio Ascendant and an Aquarian Sun. Uranus, the planet of invention and genius, was in Aries in the creative Vth.

Mark Twain wrote stories, essays and commentary for all ages in young America. He personifies the exactly rising Sun in Sagittarius, ruler of the Xth. Aries was on the Vth, and Mars and Venus were in wide conjunction in the Ist, also in Sagittarius. Mark Twain also wrote and published pornography.

Lee Harvey Oswald's Venus in Scorpio is square Pluto in Leo. Venus rules Libra, his Sun Sign. Saturn retrograde is in Aries and receives a seven-degree-orb opposition from Venus. Mars is squared by Mercury in Scorpio and is only a six-degree-orb from the square by Venus. It was published that, according to his wife, Oswald was "not a man in bed." Psychological tests bore this out and linked his aggressive actions to overcompensation for this deficient sexual profile.

Love, Relationship, Marriage, Tension

When I ponder the word love, I somehow think of Jove, Jehovah. This leads me to Jupiter. The word *love,* to my knowledge, has nothing to do etymologically with *Jove* (which goes back probably to *Yaweh*). The root of *love* is in the Old English family of words connected with *leave,* in the meaning of *permission;* i.e., "May I have your leave to . . .?" Really, love is the asking permission for relationship. One must love *something:* another person, a poem, a recipe, an opera. One establishes an emotional relationship. With another person, this relationship arises ideally with that person's permission. Love unreceived—a relationship not allowed—is indeed frustration for the giver.

The supreme love is the projection to the eternal, to a god-principle, to nature. And here we have Jove, Jehovah, Jupiter. The love of God is expansive to the infinite, embracing all of creation. Jupiter classically means expansiveness. Active expansiveness, love-in-operation, is really enthusiasm. Enthusiasm at varying levels of intensity and meaning is love.

The horoscope doesn't simply show love. The idealistic inclinations can be shown (Venus conjunct Mercury and/or the Sun; positive connections with Leo), the desire and need for love (Saturn in the XIth), the difficulty giving love (Saturn in the Vth), the mental ingredient of love (Gemini, Virgo; Mercury; IXth and IIIrd Houses), the position within world love (Pluto), and so on. When well positioned, Jupiter expands dimensions of the horoscope, brings enthusiasm and love into consideration. *Love is the identity's totality making and maintaining relationship.* The structure of the relationship, of the love, is built upon the horoscope components. The whole horoscope speaks in a totality. Is this "love at first sight"?

Most people seem to know their own Sun Sign, even though their first statement about Astrology may be negative and totally uninformed. Not only do they know their own birth Sign, they also know the Sign of their spouse and immediately offer a judgment of the two Signs' compatibility: "He's a_____and I'm a_____; and we're not supposed to go well together." Every astrologer hears this often. But have we ever heard the statement: "He's a_____and I'm a_____and boy, do we go well together!"? Rarely. A lack of information about Astrology and a fear of it keeps these people from assuming the positive dimensions of their Sign relationship one to another. They jump to empty generality to explain minor differences between them that, if they would understand a little more, could be resolved and possibly turned into complementary dimensions of separate identities.

Indeed, there are Signs that have a difficult time with one another, except in very special cases revealed only by internal examination of the horoscopes. Textbooks say that Fire (Aries, Leo, Sagittarius) "scorches" the Earth (Capricorn, Taurus, Virgo); Air (Libra, Aquarius, Gemini) "fans" the Fire; Water (Cancer, Scorpio, Pisces) "puts out" the Fire but "nurses" the Earth, and so on. Marrying within one's elemental Family, i.e., Fire to Fire, but not to the same Sign, certainly can work out very smoothly for both, allowing the partners benefits from the Cardinal-Fixed-Mutable attributes of leadership, anchor, and adaptability. But perhaps more development is attained through a more dynamic matching like Aries and Aquarius. The Aquarian husband says, "I love her fire"; the Aries wife says, "I love his steady understanding." Together they give and take, respect and grow. Each has enthusiasm for the other's uniqueness.

In a marriage between any two of the Mutable Signs (Sagittarius, Gemini, Pisces, Virgo) an important consideration might be "Who makes the decisions?"; between two Fixed Signs, "Who wins?"; between two Cardinal Signs, "Who leads?"

There are texts about all these interrelationships which describe well how decanate measurements take on important significance in marriages within the same Sign. But our point here is to show the very beginnings of understanding relationships. At a gathering about a year ago, a woman said to me, "I'm a Leo and so's my husband." (*He* was standing a deferential three feet behind her.) I simply said, "Who rules?" The short conversation turned into humor, but a year later this woman recalled this moment to me and indicated how it caused her to take stock of this powerful Leo dimension in their marriage.

Often we are asked, "What is the best Sign for me?" We're not doing our job if we just name the other two Signs in his or her triplicity or the Sign on the cusp of the Vth or VIIth. We must look further, judge the inquirer's ambition in scope and mode, as well as the sex profile. Recommending a Sun Sign must take the other factors into consideration. An Aries man with a Pisces Ascendant, or with the Moon in Pisces or even in the XIIth (which would water down his Fire considerably) might do very, very well with an Aries woman, bold and hearty, *who embodies everything he understands but can't quite externalize* in *his* personality's form.

Each Sign offers something special to a mate. Each Sign also needs something special from a relationship. At the same time, each can be said to have a "worst trait" that can show up in varying degrees in various situations. We are *not* discussing *negative types* within a Sign. Isabelle Pagan's book *From Pioneer to Poet* covers "evolved and primitive" *types* superbly. There are *traits*—syndromes of expression—in the average energy manifestation of every Sign, traits which "attract" other traits of other Signs. In a very abbreviated form, these traits stimulate traffic between the Signs, guide the "hunt" for a mate. The chart on page 160 tries to capture the best traits offered to a partner

Sign	Sex	Best trait offered to partner	Worst trait offered to partner	Trait most needed from partner
♈	male	drive, passion	overbearingness	support
	female	fire and flash	indomitability	appreciation
♉	male	stability, plan	stubbornness	assistance
	female	earthy response	egoism, temper	challenge
♊	male	bright busy-ness	indecision	anchor
	female	flexibility	superficiality	organization
♋	male	emotionality	weakness	structure
	female	sympathy	suggestibility	a cause
♌	male	regal control	tyranny	acclaim
	female	regal control	bossiness	acknowledgement
♍	male	alertness	pedantry	leadership
	female	adaptability	hypercriticalness	job assignment
♎	male	balance	wandering ego	excitement
	female	comfortable image	wandering ego	adoration
♏	male	deep needs	secretiveness	patience
	female	deep response	schemingness	attention
♐	male	spirit and effort	closed-mindedness	depth
	female	enthusiasm	opinionatedness	direction
♑	male	leadership, responsibility	moroseness	receptivity
	female	strength	unemotionality	creativity
♒	male	bright confidence	arrogance	appreciation
	female	unusual talent	eccentricity	opportunity
♓	male	flexibility	languidness	stimulation
	female	receptivity	passiveness	leadership

by a man or by a woman of a given Sign; the trait most needed from a partner by a man or by a woman in a given Sign; and the possible worst traits for each in the process of making and maintaining relationships. Of course, these abbreviations are tiny pebbles from a mountain, but they do tell us about the region. This table may be helpful as a guide to answering the question, "What Sign is best for me?" Of course, having the horoscope of one or both parties in a relationship can tell the story quite accurately.

The chart on page 162 is that of a female television producer, divorced, who had been seeing a man fourteen years younger than she for some time. Comparison of the two charts showed that the relationship was excellent intellectually and sexually. Conversation corroborated this. The woman was an Aries with much executive drive and sexual fire (Sun, Venus, and Uranus in triple conjunction in Aries in the Xth). Her elevated Mercury in Pisces, also in the Xth, trine to a rising Cancer Pluto (ruler of Scorpio intercepted in the Vth) kept her indomitability in line; i.e., she "knew" she couldn't enjoy the pleasures of the relationship—any relationship—if she were overbearing, especially with the age difference. The Piscean effect upon Mercury "waters down" much of the mental fire. Additionally, Sun-Uranus-Venus squared *Saturn on the VIIth cusp.* —Here could have been (and was) a life-long difficulty with men, who were always younger or older by far than she, and lessons learned after a divorce.

She wanted appreciation most from her partner. The young man certainly was grateful for and appreciative of her attention. His Sun was in Scorpio (deep needs) and he expected patience from his mate, patience for his grand plan. The native described how the young man wanted to go to a foreign country after his higher education ended, and take her with him. The man was nearing twenty-eight; Saturn's return would structure plans

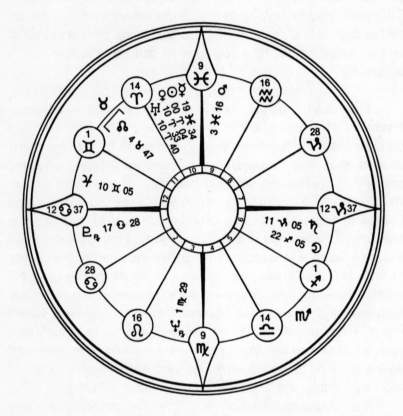

indeed. His secretiveness kept many details from this woman. The question was, "Should I go with him?"

The fourteen to fifteen years difference in their ages gave them opposing Saturn positions, bringing his birth Saturn to an opposition with hers, therefore conjunct *her* Ascendant! His ambition would overrule her whole personality, especially since the return of Saturn to its birth position in his life would correspond to the Saturn *transit* of *her* Ascendant! —The native should enjoy the situation, prepare for a peak in her own life, and encourage his new life direction to come—without her. She would have her own new preparations to undertake.

Marriage of course brings the pebbles back to the mountain, and the whole of horoscopy comes into focus. It is at times of tension or divorce, however, that the "worst traits" come into focus. Warning of this and suggesting antidotes can save much sorrow and misunderstanding. With no intention to be humorous in abbreviation, some vignette observations can show the direction of fuller counsel that can be enormously helpful, guided by the trait table on page 160.

- Never discuss emotional problems with a Piscean at night. Fatigue brings passivity into focus, and frustration follows because no progress is made.
- Never interrupt an Aries who is trying to make an emotional point. When through—exhausted—the Arian will respect your appreciation of Arian passion and fire.
- Always help the Taurus to see Taurus' way. This assistance will usually bring about instinctive concession.
- Be prepared to absorb nervous criticism before the Gemini gets to the point. Explain the alternative side quickly.
- When a Cancer dissolves into tears, create some diversion related to a new goal, a new topic.

- With a stressed Leo, submit and then request permission and guidance for describing the other side of the matter.
- Dot all the "i's" and cross all "t's" with a Virgo in tension. Get the story straight and, if possible, bring in outside leadership.
- With Libra, appeal to the sense of justice and social image through flattery and objectifying the problem.
- Be patient with the Scorpio. Let Scorpio discover the meanings of the situation alone. Keep the lights on and all discussion open.
- Try to show new dimensions, significant depths of the problem, to the tense Sagittarian.
- Cheer up the Capricorn with spontaneous creativity, encouraging the Capricorn to see his or her self humorously.
- Appreciate the Aquarian's inspiration and unique views. Create new opportunities to guide energies under stress into other areas.

The ambition and sex profiles of the horoscope intertwine continuously. Ambition needs creative fuel, and sex (sociability, copulation, cultural appreciation, etc.) boosts self-awareness and self-esteem toward ambition's goal. Priorities form within time structure. Psychology (Abraham Maslow) has established a hierarchy of needs. Every identity shares the same needs. Tension among needs changes levels of fulfillment, and the identity develops.

Modern times expect change. Identities must put on coats of many colors. The heterogeneity of every identity is its claim to fame in a world of many, many more people and many, many more specialization possibilities than ever before. The horoscope depicts the fabric and weave of the identity's mantle.

Love is the projection of the identity. It is involved with enthusiasm in work, establishing relationships, as well as communication with God. Our identity loves with different motives, in different modes, expecting relationships and the return of love in equally as many forms: from a job promotion to the inspiration of the spirit.

The grandeur of the whole transcends the acute drama of the specific. Problems demand perspective before solution is possible. Because a situation has little or no value of its own, it is our reaction to it that gives value and potential. The architect sees the whole in a private perspective, but he must "realize" the creative building blocks in order to stand strong, construct fulfillment of a dream, and serve his world.

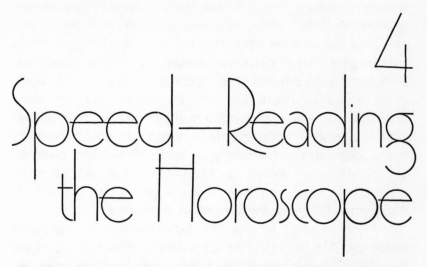

Speed–Reading the Horoscope

4

The flash of identity recognition that we experience so often, the momentary awareness of whole identities, can be applied in relative measure to reading the horoscope, the blueprint of the whole. For some extraordinarily gifted astrologers perhaps there is the gift to read a birth map immediately, in that "flash." And for others, a succession of detailed measurements easily clogs up inspired understanding. There are techniques that can be helpful in speeding up awareness of the horoscope.

Often this book talks about seeing analysis quickly and easily. This by no means is to say that the art of synthesis is a quick and easy matter. We all labor long and hard over many horoscopes. With experience, though, certain abbreviated techniques evolve to help us get to the key more quickly. With experience we learn to trust the first impressions more when they are grounded upon tried and tested techniques. Modern times press us to perform swiftly and in quantity. Individual horoscopes used to be presented in book form, literally! Now—unfortunately one can get a "flash-horoscope" from a computer, while in a train station rushing somewhere. Emergencies arise that require the astrologer to write "the book" in a flash!

With the thousands of measurements possible in any

horoscope, with highly individualized and painstakingly evolved systems like Witte's Hamburg School of midpoints, extra planets, etc., like the Arabian Parts and the parts created by modern astrologers, like primary directions, tertiary directions, embolismic lunations, solar revolutions, etc.—we sometimes don't know where to begin. But one beacon emerges: for some dimension to be very meaningful in the horoscope, there always seem to be several measurements pointing to the *same* dimension, trait, potential event. As soon as these deductions begin to accumulate, to corroborate one another, we know we are close to a key. Then, we know how to focus more detailed search to discover the full story, the motivation, the energy.

Much of what follows may be elementary to established astrologers. Maybe not! These abbreviations, these techniques, *are* helpful and will illuminate avenues into and out from the complications the horoscope embodies. Additionally, reliance upon mental deduction will help exercise the mind and rest the pencil!

The Sun Sign. Astrologers are often put on the spot: "Tell me something about myself." Unless the Sun Sign is extraordinarily obvious—and when it is, one can even hypothesize the decanate and come to a "guessed" calendar day of birth which can be dramatic indeed—no astrologer should risk the guess. I've made many mistakes, trusting my observations too much, too quickly, and doing nothing for Astrology or myself by "entertainingly" failing in a guess. But I have had some dramatic successes, done purely on speedy deduction. Having to do this is often part of what is socially expected of an astrologer. He can get out of it easily, but the temptation to prove something is always there. Here are two examples that actually happened, spontaneously and ever so dramatically.

The man was the head of the music department at a university. His physical appearance was so Aries as not to be believed: fiery red hair, flushed complexion, slightly pointed chin, lean build, tremendous energy, and such a nervous drive to get on with things that much of what he did lacked quality. He had the tremendous Aries knack for forgetting personal failings, so the lack of quality in his work or the social disruption his passionate drive caused was easily cast out of awareness. He spoke so fast and intensely that his very words perspired, and sentences climbed all over one another. The man was a dynamo and extremely valuable in his job for the grand enthusiasm and leadership he generated and transmitted. One or two meetings with him filled out the picture, but instantly, on first meeting, one would record these impressions easily.

Eventually, the question came: "Well, what Sign am I?" The immediate answer, always with the protection and courtesy of a question mark: "Aries?" Right. —Well, I suppose you can tell me the day too?" A moment's thought: he is the head of a department, structuring music, drama, education. The decanates of Aries (of any Sign) are a procession of the elemental family Signs, ten days or ten degrees each, starting always with the birth Sign and proceeding through the successive modes (Cardinal, Fixed, Mutable, Cardinal, etc.). For Aries, this would be Aries, the first ten days of the Aries Month (March 21 to March 31) and the first ten degrees of Aries; then the second decanate's (or decant's) group of days and degrees, with sub-characteristics of a Leo nature, April 1 to April 10; then the third decanate of twenty degrees through thirty degrees Aries, April 11 to April 20, with sub-characteristics of Sagittarius.

The man was in education . . . the Sagittarius decanate? But he was also head of the department . . . the Leo decanate? His manner really was that of a fiery leader demanding recognition more through position and radiation than through thought and academic disciplines. The odds were on the Leo decanate, April 1 to April 10. I took the midpoint, April 5, and suggested, with humor and again with courtesy to his "right" to whatever day he was born, "April 5?" —That remark made local "history." He was born April 6.

On another occasion, I was new to a community, and people were just learning about "the astrologer." I went to an athletic event with some friends and began chatting with a woman on the sidelines. She had a powerful, stocky, yet not unattractive build. Her complexion was "earthy." She had a subtle beauty reflected in her clothes and words, a good laugh which somehow showed stability and real temper potential in the background. Then the question: "What's my Sign?" I replied with a seemingly unrelated question, trying to corroborate, even in the slightest way, my strong impression of Taurus: "Is your favorite color turquoise [Venus' color]?" She said that it was! I said Taurus and was right. "Oh, that's because I'm built like a bull, like my husband says! Can you tell the date too?"

The decanates for Taurus proceed in order through the family, as we have seen, starting with the birth Sign: Taurus, April 21 to April 30, first decanate; May 1 to May 10, second decanate with Virgo sub-characteristics; May 10 to May 20, the third decanate with Capricorn sub-characteristics.

Her conversation had had a lot of implicit and outspoken little criticisms in it, about the event, the area, general life. This would suggest the Virgo decanate. She was dressed totally in brown with little touches of orange in her pins, jewelry, etc. This is another corroboration of the Virgo (decanate), through rulership by Mercury and Mercury's rust-color. I chose the midpoint of this second decanate and said "May 5?" It was May 4. This deduction also made history and my introduction to the area got off to a flying start!

These deductive "games" illustrate the enormous power the Signs and their degree groupings have *in generating a surface trait,* a pebble from the mountain, that speaks in a flash about the whole. Thoughts about this potential can exercise the perceptions and understandings of the astrologer. Use of them creates significant social and professional rewards. Speedreading the horoscope really is—begins with—speedreading the person. —Try improving flash deductions by understanding how they can be constructed. Speed and reliability improve rapidly. If the flash is clear immediately, pursue it. If it isn't clear, abandon it; the situation is not so externally manifested.

The Ascendant. Our minds make Sun-Sign deductions all the time. Eventually corroboration is received by question or by the person volunteering the information. If the actual Sun Sign seems to contradict the initial mental deduction, we know there is powerful planetary and/or Ascendant influence directly manifested. For example, if a Capricorn is a fiery dynamo and perhaps has red hair, flushed complexion , etc., it is justifiable to assume that he was born with an Aries Ascendant. That would mean he was born between 10:00 A.M. and Noon, "around Noon." The chart on page 172 illustrates how this deduction, the deduction of the Ascendant determined by birth time, can be made in any number of instances (this procedure can also be utilized as an excellent mental exercise in perception).

The wheel of the horoscope contains 360 degrees, traversed by the Sun in twenty-four hours, two hours per House division. The Signs arrange themselves around the wheel in monthly divisions. The Sun position by Sign is determined by calendar birth date. The Sun's position by *House* division is determined by local clock birth time.

The latitude of birthplace is an important variable for the size of the Houses and does affect the Sun's House position somewhat. With experience, one learns at which latitudes (around which major cities) interceptions often occur, allowing one to refine a mental deduction a bit further. But following this time scheme described below narrows the choice of Ascendant to two Signs at most; usually one becomes obvious, and the corresponding birth time can be accurately approximated.

Needless to say, this is a very important first aid in rectification.

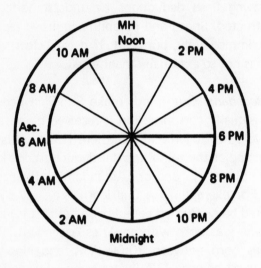

The Capricorn with such obvious Aries characteristics would be born near noon because that is where Capricorn falls by the time-division of the Houses, *when Aries is on the Ascendant.* If he were a Libra with Aries characteristics, he would probably have been born in late afternoon, between four and six. Libra is the polar opposite to Aries and to place Aries on the Ascendant is to place Libra on the VIIth. A Capricorn with a Cancer Ascendant would be born similarly in late afternoon, because to put Cancer on the Ascendant is to place Capricorn on the VIIth.

A final example: a Gemini with many of the heavy, silent, severe characteristics of a certain type of Capricorn might very well have a Capricorn Ascendant. Putting Capricorn on the Ascendant would put the opposite Sign Cancer on the VIIth. Gemini is one sign behind Cancer and would be on the VIth. This is where the Sun would be between 6 and 8 P.M., in Gemini with a Capricorn Ascendant.

Further deductions can follow immediately when sufficient corroboration is gleaned, or in an effort to corroborate the House arrangement through questions. A mental image of the cuspal arrangement can be achieved with practice, by rotating the imaginary wheel to a Capricorn Ascendant and "seeing" Aquarius on the IInd, Pisces on the IIIrd, Aries on the IVth, Taurus on the Vth, Gemini on the VIth, etc. A Sun in the VIth with a Capricorn Ascendant generally would suggest strong administrative and work ability, mentally oriented; probably more respect and attention to detail, consciously cultivated, than is usual for the mercurial Gemini. There might be some unusual income situation (Aquarius on the IInd), and the native might well attract relationships with, or benefit from emotional traits of, the Cancerian (on the VIIth cusp). The sex profile is probably quite secret and "earthy"—much more so than in the usual Gemini horoscope—because of Taurus on the Vth and Scorpio on the XIth. And so on.

If the further deductions don't gain corroboration, stop. There's probably an interception and if correction can't be made mentally, the exercise value of the observations is gone. Then there is only confusion.

If things seem to "click," there may be important transits occurring at that moment over angles, and important specifics can be offered. For example: in May, 1972, a keenly sharp female executive I met at a party asked about her Sign and details. She was about fifty-five, extremely forthright and attractive, but had never been married. She worked as an editor of a corporation publication.

She volunteered that she was a Sagittarian. The deduction that she might have a Virgo Ascendant was easy to make; highly refined critical ability, language skill, editorial profession, never married, meticulously groomed. A Virgo Ascendant would put Sagittarius (her birth Sign) on the IVth; the angles normally square one another by Sign in the procession of Signs. This would put a publishing-communication emphasis on her X-IV "professional" axis (Gemini-Sagittarius) and corroborate her occupation. With Sagittarius on the IVth, giving her the Virgo Ascendant, she would have had a birth time of "around midnight."

In May, 1972, Saturn and Mars had just separated from a very important transit conjunction early in Gemini. This conjunction would have taken place on her Gemini (opposite Sagittarius) Midheaven! We know that Saturn at the Midheaven often means a grand culmination of professional effort. (Neptune was in opposition to this transit on the woman's IVth.) I submitted that perhaps in the last three months she had been promoted in her job or given some conspicuous honor. She was overwhelmed. She had been made senior management representative to a special committee that was prestigious throughout the major international company. Then she hastily added, "But the job isn't really such an honor." Neptune near her Sun in the IVth? Gemini Saturn going on a bit farther to oppose her Sagittarian Sun . . . frustration?

Another example of things "clicking" occurred just a few weeks later in a restaurant. I joined some friends at another table for a moment and was introduced to their guest as "our friend, the astrologer." Shortly after initial greetings, the guest impulsively offered his birth date and time: "May 26, I'm a Gemini, born at 9:34 in the evening." Obviously, I was to perform some miracle then and there, and this time, a "miracle" would indeed be easy: between 8 and 10 P.M., the native would probably have his Gemini Sun in the Vth House, probably giving an Aquarius Ascendant. The guest was a very successful designer, highly intense, and my intuition and certain other observations suggested that he was a homosexual. The very same Mars-Saturn transit conjunction used in the preceding example would have occurred *conjunct his Sun* in the first week of April, 1972. One could expect a peak of fulfillment in his creative life (transit Saturn conjunct Sun in the Vth) and perhaps in his sex life as well (Mars involved; Vth House). Scorpio was probably on the Midheaven (sex *in* business?). These deductions made in about five to ten seconds, I replied that perhaps he had had quite a dramatic, important time in his business and sex lives early in April, perhaps big problems from mixing them. The guest was astounded: to him it *was* a "miracle."

The Saturn Skeleton. We have already seen many examples of Saturn's orbit by quadrature. Many times in lectures and at casual social gatherings, when the topic of Astrology arises, I simply observe aloud that there is probably no one in the room whose life didn't take a new level, a new path between twenty-six and thirty. Of course, this allows considerable leeway, but also provides an introduction to an explanation of the Saturn cycle that says a great deal for Astrology and its time structure and for the importance of getting counsel at the most important times of ambition's growth.

On our mental wheel, we can also insert a general Saturn position. We know Saturn stays in one Sign about two to two-and-one-half years. In the case of the editor (page 173), at about fifty-five years of age, her Saturn was about two Signs away from its second return. At the moment of our conversation, Saturn was in early Gemini, in her Xth. Two Signs more, when she will be near sixty, Saturn will return to its place, probably early in the XIIth (two Houses from the Xth, scene of the present transit) in Leo, heading for the Virgo Ascendant. This would corroborate many of the deductions already made and bring up many others. And all this can happen during about thirty seconds to a minute of calm conversation!

Last winter, a German stagehand at an opera house came up to me in the canteen. He was very handsome and in his early forties. He said he needed his horoscope done but couldn't afford it; he had a limp and said he was a Capricorn born just before midnight. This would have given Capricorn on the IVth cusp and a Libra Ascendant, corroborated by his handsome appearance, his work in an artistic firm, and other observations. Saturn at that moment was in early Gemini and Uranus was in middle Libra. Counting back through the Signs to when he was around twenty-eight, about twelve-and-a-half years, would put his radical Saturn in late Sagittarius, in the IIIrd House. The man was earnest. I submitted some deductions, planning to stop immediately, of course, should any one of them be off base.

The pronounced limp in the upper part of his leg led me to assume that Saturn in Sagittarius, for this Capricorn, was a very sensitive planetary position, undoubtedly involved in a debilitating configuration that climaxed perhaps upon Saturn's first return. I asked if he had injured his leg or had been very ill near twenty-eight. He replied that he had contracted polio at that time. This was in the IIIrd House, I was assuming, the House of brothers and sisters as well. I asked if something had happened to his brother or sister at that same time. He replied that his brother had died at the same time. Uranus probably had recently transited the Libra Ascendant: I asked if he had changed his home within the last year, significantly. He said that he had. I asked if the home change had also involved a separation from his wife (Libra, marriage). He replied this time, by this time with tears in his eyes, that he had indeed separated from his wife.

All the deductions were right, and we were then able to talk more sensitively about his situation, especially knowing that Saturn was rising to his Midheaven.

This unusual exchange was recalled vividly to me last month. I was at a party given by quite an international millionaire. I was introduced to a striking Middle-Eastern woman in a golden Sari whose name was Princess_____. She immediately began to talk about Astrology, saying that her family's court had had astrologers ever since she could remember, and that a full horoscope had been made for her upon her birth. I estimated her age in the early forties and quick calculation, as in the preceding example, placed her Saturn in Sagittarius also. She volunteered that she was a Leo and offered her exact birthtime, which I can't recall, but which would place her Sun near the IInd cusp, giving her a late Cancer Ascendant. That meant that Saturn in Sagittarius would fall very near her VIth cusp, perhaps in the Vth, perhaps in the VIth. She was testing me, very obviously. She said that the court astrologers had predicted that she would have many children, but that she had none and was then unmarried. Again, I felt that her Saturn was probably problematic in her chart, in her Vth or VIth. She then asked if I could add any more to that—then and there! I remembered the stagehand I had talked with last winter and said that perhaps throughout her life she had had problems with her upper leg and hip. The deduction, the hunch was right! Then, she asked about the future: her age suggested that a "second adolescence" was coming with the Saturn opposition to its own place, closely followed within the next two years by the Saturn transit of her Ascendant. These observations brought a twinkle to her eye; the Princess was pleased and surely already had plans of her own!

Working with the chart

After we construct the chart, our real work begins. The mind can wobble at the prospect of analyzing the myriad measurements. What can we do quickly to help us find a key?

Sun-Venus rapport. We have already discussed this on page 120, and it is an invaluable beginning, especially with a female. In the horoscope I did for a client this morning, the Sun-Venus rapport was precisely forty-five degrees. The woman was approaching her forty-fifth birthday. Her birth Venus in the Ist squared Saturn (one degree orb) in the IVth. The progressed Sun would square Saturn just before conjoining Venus, this next year, while transiting Saturn crossed her Ascendant. The key to her anxiety was found in a flash.

Sun-Mars rapport. The significance of this approximate measurement is keenest when Mars is the ruling planet of the Sun Sign or Ascendant, or extremely prominent. For a woman, the conjunction, sextile, or trine can be a time that corresponds to marriage, if the Sun-Venus rapport timing is "impractical." The square especially can mark a detail—important or incidental—the effect of which covers two years sometimes. For example, my own Mars is strongly marked but is not dominant. When my Sun progressed close to a conjunction with my Mercury, square to Mars' birth position, I had two minor but familially disruptive auto scrapes at seventeen years of age (seventeen degrees). When the conjunction with Mercury was completed, I began college travel activity, over 80,000 miles in four years. In situations where the VIth or XIIth House is involved, this rapport measurement (Sun square Mars) often can mark a time of hospitalization and/or operation, depending on other indices.

Sun-Saturn rapport. My Saturn is in the Xth opposed by Neptune in the IVth. My Capricorn Sun is in the VIIth. (Immediately this information should spin the reader's mental wheel: we know that I must have been born in 1935 or 1936, when this opposition took place with Saturn in Pisces and Neptune in Virgo. Immediately we know that, with a VIIth House Capricorn Sun, I was born in late afternoon, and probably have a late Gemini or early Cancer Ascendant, etc.) When my Sun progressed to a sextile with Saturn in seven years, and a trine to Neptune, there was much change in my home. My father left the family and the man who was to become my stepfather entered the picture and saved a very sorry situation. Yes, with Saturn in the Midheaven at birth, it would cross the Ascendant in about seven years. Would the Ascendant be Cancer instead of

Gemini, accenting the home situation still further and implying an interception, since the Ascendant would then trine the *Pisces* Xth?

The woman whose horoscope is on page 180 has the Sun in Aries exactly on the Midheaven. Saturn is in Capricorn in the VIth, opposing Jupiter, Pluto, and Mars, all in Cancer in the XIIth. Uranus and Mercury are in wide Aries conjunction in the Xth squaring Pluto in the XIIth and Saturn in the VIth. Think. This would show the skeleton of home restriction (Cancer and XIIth), sickness and confinement (aspects relating VIth, XIIth, and Saturn, with Mercury and Uranus in Aries), as well as nervous tension and perhaps breakaway (Uranus). When the Sun progressed fifteen degrees by approximate one-year-equals-one-degree rapport measurement, it would be square to Saturn and perhaps awaken this whole complex. It did: the native was a nervous wreck, confined to her home after hospitalization, restricted terribly, was in a wheelchair for some of the time—and ran away from home! Yes, Saturn had transited to the opposition of its birth place and was nearing the Ascendant. —This measurement was the key to a very complicated childhood emotional legacy compounded by chronic sickness and a totally deaf father.

Sun-Uranus rapport. What wonderful times when the Sun progresses to trine or sextile with the birth position of Uranus! In the horoscope on page 32, the trine to Uranus would be at seven degrees Leo just about to leave the Vth House. The native's Sun would progress there in thirty-two to thirty-three degrees, at age thirty-two to thirty-three. (Saturn would have just made its first return and be one-and-a-half Signs further along, i.e., returned to its place in Sagittarius—we know what that means—at the Midheaven—we know that too—and have gone on into its own Sign, Capricorn, in the XIth, hopes and wishes, friends, love received. Would this time have been the best time of her life, a

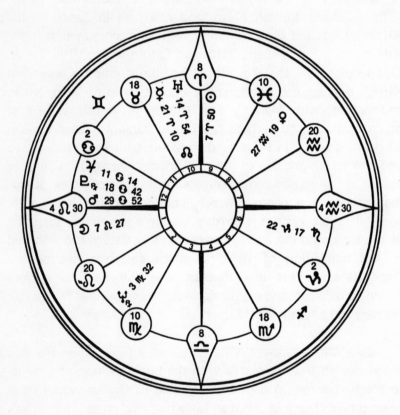

time of children, dreams? It was: the native gave birth to two children, fulfilled her Cancer Sun's motherhood dream, but, since the Sun was approaching the VIth, the enthusiasm of fulfillment began to project itself to new forms of service and work. The inactivity of the mind was highlighted, the good times brought fresh incentives. The native would be preparing for Saturn's build-up to the Ascendant transit.

When the Sun progresses to the square of Uranus, this is a classic aspect of separation and tension. It is not necessarily correlated with divorce—though so often this *is* the case—but it can certainly mean geographical displacement through tension created in areas of the life marked by the bodies' House positions.

The woman whose horoscope was discussed on page 85 will undergo this square this year. She is an American who was living in Germany who has just turned thirty. We studied her horoscope together one-and-a-half years ago. In the period of the square, Uranus would transit the Ascendant and, of course, Saturn would have made its first return, and in the birth chart, Saturn and Uranus were in conjunction in the VIIIth. The family was secure, happy, successful. Very carefully, I tried to prepare her to manage the disruptive tensions and decisions ahead.

Of course, a housewife, under such conditions as these especially, has little outlet for the energies: she is subject to her husband's career assignments, his development. *With no outlet through him,* the tensions would bring upheaval *in* the home. It was essential to deduce something quickly in relation to this period from the husband's horoscope.

That was easy! The husband would have Saturn in transit over his IVth cusp at the beginning of the same time period: a new beginning for him, perhaps some new job, certainly a new home, or at least a promotion or dislocation. (It turned out that he too asked for his horoscope analysis. His major question was, "When might I expect a promotion?"

When Saturn did cross his IVth, he got a promotion and was called back to the United States. The actual move was delayed four months, while the wife had another baby, exactly when Uranus crossed her Ascendant! Saturn was still to return to its own position in the wife's chart (conjunct Uranus and Saturn) four months later. This could well be the state of affairs that would bring a change of direction for the wife and give her much needed focus upon other dimensions in her life shown by the rest of the horoscope.

Three months later, the family was again relocated to the Middle East. One month later, as Saturn returned in the VIIIth and the very sensitive point there (Uranus with Saturn ruled the Aquarian Vth, children, creativity), the native underwent a deep emotional shift, seeking her identity in a new land, a land deeply significant to her past and philosophical readings, and she had a difficult miscarriage, requiring surgery (the VIIIth is the fourth of the Vth).

The progressed square to Uranus by the Sun is still mounting. Will her new "way" ease the tensions of such geographic and emotional dislocation? Of course there are other dimensions here, but the important instruction for these pages is the interweaving of tensions and release within time. No pencil was needed to make the deductions above. To qualify them, yes, but seeing where to go with analysis, seizing the key of the moment quickly was done swiftly and efficiently.

A special note must be made here about these progressed movements of the Sun. I have referred to them as "rapport" measurements, since they are made by quick approximation. Dane Rudhyar covers this subject so well in *Astrology of Personality*, applying rapport measurements to all bodies in the horoscope, one degree per year; and Sepharial applied an expanded radix system of analysis. When working with the other planets, the procedure can become very complicated: again we come up with many different measurements. *Seeing* the rapport measurements between the other bodies is as easy as seeing them with the Sun and is indeed worthwhile, especially for corroboration of psychological situations and/or major events and trends. Giving special attention to the Sun comes closest to the heart of the Secondary Progression premise, using the Sun's motion of nearly one degree per day (year) as the base of life energy development throughout life in time.

The Sun progresses a *little less* than one degree every day (year). We know this and, after thirty years (easy to remember), the approximately two-minute lag in daily (yearly) motion behind an exact degree accumulates *to a full degree,* sixty minutes. So around thirty years of age, we should make a mental correction, adding an extra year (day) for development; and at sixty, still another, making a two-degree delay overall that we must consider then. For example, the woman enjoying the Sun progressed to trine position with Uranus, page 179, gave confirmation of the deduction but commented that thirty-four more than likely was the highpoint! Here was that one degree (one year) accumulation.

These rapport measurements are accomplished swiftly, inspire excellent questions for the client with which to begin dialogue, and keynote major life-energy application potentials within time. The progressions by and large reflect the *internal state* of the native, the potential reactions, the needs; the coincidental transits indicate *environmental press and events* which trigger the reactions. *And all must echo the definition of the identity and the thrust of the birth plan.*

Retrogradation and direct motion stations. The eye can ever so quickly note when, in the progressed life, a planet retrograde at birth will make its *station* (seem stationary) and assume direct motion; when a planet in direct motion at birth will make its station and take on retrograde motion.

The example on page 133, the "call from Paris," shows this easily: the husband's Sun had progressed to a square with his Saturn; the wife's Sun, to a square of her Jupiter in her VIIth. Immediately one knew that both were under tension: his Saturn, ruler of the Xth and in his XIIth, obviously could suggest a major job tension, ambition restricted, etc. The Scorpio Sun in the VIIIth suggested the depths of his concern and, later, led to the internal struggle he was having to distill the way and direction of his ambition (Saturn in Pisces opposing Neptune). He was thirty-five, near a repeat of Saturn's second time around on its first square to its own position. But in the Ephemeris, Mercury took on retrograde motion at thirty-five! This was corroboration enough to establish a key for deeper analysis: the native obviously had finally established a *mental* counterpoint, a new theme, related to his deeply private efforts to fulfill ambition, and the identity was expressing itself in enormous job tension and the threat of professional separation. Might he finally be able to go into business for himself?

When Venus goes retrograde, an emotional counterpoint may establish itself, often a frustration factor in the areas ruled by Venus in the birth chart. When Mars goes retrograde, energy gets "backed up" through application to another theme, the counterpoint. Jupiter suggests a change of greater fortunes, an alteration of the applications of enthusiasm; Saturn, a shift in ambition and its significance for the identity.

When these planets are retrograde at birth and assume direct motion in the progressed life, the counterpoint is abandoned, the planetary values manifest themselves more directly, more easily; ground already covered is gone over again, mistakes can be corrected, new perspectives attained. Love takes on less complicated expression, flows more easily; the mind and thinking process can become more flexible or apply themselves more efficiently or directly to problems; often long-time inferiority feelings are dropped and ambition moves more quickly.

The corresponding manifestations are not swift or dramatic. They are undercurrents to change that flow through two or three years of the life, easily supporting the manifestations of important progressed aspects and transits. —When the station occurs in conjunction with a birth planet's position or in clear aspect to an important body, naturally the meaning is intensified.

The Midheaven. The Midheaven progresses very nearly one degree every year and is always the same distance from the progressed Sun as the radical Midheaven is from the radical Sun. Just adding the years of life to the Midheaven progresses the point. This is really a kind of quick abbreviation of the primary directions that bring a planet in the southeast quadrant (X, XI, XII) up to the Midheaven.

The native with Xth House Saturn opposed by Neptune in the IVth, suggesting early disruption in the home, one or both parents taken from the scene, underwent the Midheaven progression to conjunction with this opposition axis at ten years of age. Was there trouble in the home between seven and ten years of age (Saturn would have come to the Ascendant in about seven years, remember)? Yes, there was: the father walked out when the native was nine, after three years of chaos.

In the example on page 181, the woman undergoing extensive relocation, the Midheaven comes to a conjunction with the Xth House Mars at thirty-one, the time of her great stress and shift through her husband's job, children, public orientation. Mars rules her Aries VIIth, her husband, from the Xth, her social position and his new beginning (fourth of the VIIth), as well as the "end of the matter" concerning him; in wide opposition to her Moon isolated in the IVth, the home, ruler of the Cancer Xth.

Converse progression of the Midheaven also can afford corroboration of other observations. A man has Uranus in the XIth, hopes and wishes for individual expression, in Taurus. The

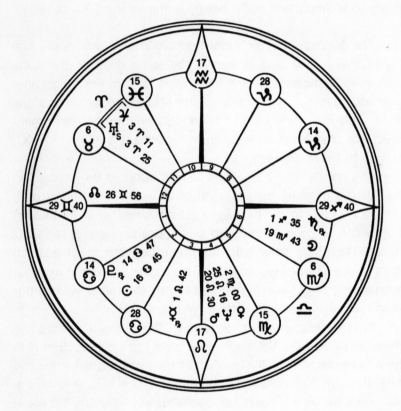

birth Uranus is trined by the birth Sun and Jupiter in the VIIth, relating this expression to the public with excellent good fortune. Venus, ruler of Taurus, the Sign holding Uranus, is in the IXth in Aquarius! These two planets are in *mutual reception,* each in the Sign of the other's rulership. Though not in aspect, there is a strong rapport between them.

The native is a public performer and wanted to follow his Venus profession in a foreign country (IXth). At thirty-two, converse progression of the Midheaven would have gone backward from 7 Pisces to 5 Aquarius and squared the birth Uranus from Uranus' own Sign. Might this be corroboration of other dimensions—a tension in the professional X-IV axis and highly individual hopes and wishes (Uranus in the XIth) related to foreign countries through Venus in the IXth, a tension that suddenly (Uranus) would correspond to a job shift and a unique orientation? It was.

The woman whose horoscope appears on page 186 has a 17 Aquarius Midheaven and Jupiter at 3 Aries intercepted in the XIth. The distance is forty-six degrees (years). Her Venus is in 2 Virgo in the IVth, a very sensitive point in this horoscope. The *converse* progression of the Midheaven to the trine with the birth Venus would be to 2 Capricorn in her VIIth, a distance of forty-five degrees (years). The rapport measurement of the Sun to conjunction with this Venus is forty-six degrees (and one degree-year fewer to the square with Saturn!)—be cautious about adding the one degree around thirty. The native came to the astrologer twenty days before her forty-fifth birthday (Saturn would have been making its second opposition to its own place)! The key years were certainly delineated; the concerns about romance, life fortune, marriage, life-long dreams, social honor, home were all involved dramatically.

In the example described on page 135, the husband has a Midheaven of 6 Capricorn. He was thirty-five at the time of the inquiry, bringing the Midheaven to 11 Aquarius in his XIth, hopes and wishes, exactly square his Taurus Uranus in the Ist, indicating a job shift arising out of tension about expression of long-held hopes and wishes. The *converse* Midheaven from 6 Capricorn (minus thirty-five degrees) comes to 1 Sagittarius, conjunct his radical Mercury (just turned retrograde in progression), trine to Pluto in the Vth (creativity), sextile to the birth Mars in the XIth. He was surely thinking about new public outlets (Pluto) for his creativity, experiencing a creative tension about individual expression through the profession.

Planetary movements. Much of this book deals with Saturn's period of twenty-eight to thirty years, the time Saturn takes to complete one orbit back to its birth position. Of course, the time of the planetary orbit is always slightly irregular because of retrogradation, but knowledge of the general orbit is always useful, as we have seen with Saturn. Checking the Ephemeris is indispensable, but in speedreading the horoscope to find the key for deeper concentration of our analysis, knowledge of the movement cycles is extremely useful and helpful. And often astrologers must work very quickly, on-the-spot, at critical moments. It is not unusual that a marriage argument brings a "house-call," once memorably three hours before the couple's joint or separate departure on international flights to togetherness or separation.

When Jupiter enters the birth Sign, good prospects are usually ahead, especially when Jupiter transits conjunct the birth Sun. Of course, this can be more complicated if either Jupiter or Sun is in tension in the birth chart of if progressions and transits at the same time suggest difficulty or delay in reaction. By and large, however, much can be gained in analysis by being aware of Jupiter's twelve-year period.

Jupiter covers one Sign in approximately one year, thirty degrees a year, almost three degrees a month. Immediately, some hope of a change of fortune can be offered a client in a moment of tension or sorrow if a projection of Jupiter's movement will make a favorable relationship in the horoscope soon.

Here is an example: the native was twenty-three years and seven months old, three years out of college, in the wandering, last quadrant of ambition's (Saturn's) first orbit. The shifts were being made that would climax with Saturn's return four or five years later. In the birth chart, Jupiter was closely conjunct the Sun in the VIIth, a very favorable position. But, at the moment of inquiry, between jobs and without work and money after a big move, his enormous ambition as yet not focused, the native was extraordinarily depressed. But Jupiter was to return to its own place near the Sun for the second time (the first at twelve) at twenty-four. The Ephemeris indicated a Jupiter transit of Jupiter's birth position at twenty-three years and eleven months, conjunct the Sun at twenty-four. In the difficult period, Jupiter had been retrograde for five months: the fortunes had indeed been in "counterpoint." The native had been precociously successful, but the fortunes turned around somehow.

In great despondency, after perhaps fifty job interviews in one month, sacrificing his individuality and dreams, he took a stop-gap job and was to start work at twenty-three years and nine months. But checking the Ephemeris, it is seen that *Saturn* transited the Sun in retrograde motion and turned direct at this time (two months before Jupiter would arrive), a time when one would expect freedom of ambition, fulfillment of dreams, and establishment of good fortune (Jupiter) for perhaps a twelve-year period. Nine days before the exact station of Saturn, the native received a telephone call out of the blue in the line of specialized work in which he had given up hope of employment. An interview produced immediate employment. Within the first week he enjoyed a significant promotion to a different department in the firm and thirteen weeks later, just before his twenty-fourth birthday, with Jupiter returned to *its* birth position and the Sun, still another corporate shift to an exceedingly rewarding position! —And Saturn was climbing toward its birth position in the Xth. There was another shift at that time, into an entirely new profession.

At twelve years of age, when Jupiter made its first return to its birth position (and, in this case, the Sun), the native also had a shift in fortunes. At twelve, the "fortunes" were tied to school and family experiences, of course. He was very unhappy at a public school, and his parents decided to make arrangements for his admission to an illustrious private school. The native began in the new school the following fall, exactly when *Saturn* came to his IVth cusp, a new beginning, and spent one year back and forth in opposition to its birth position, when the native was thirteen-and-a-half to fourteen-and-a-half. Jupiter had returned to its birth position and the Sun as well. This change of fortunes was indeed critical and affected the native's ambition and education until he was out of college at twenty-one.

It is helpful to note that two-and-a-half Jupiter orbits approximate one Saturn orbit. Understandably, a stressing of fortunes, an awareness of the fortune conditions, needs, and potentials can often stimulate a change in the level and/or direction of ambition. The Jupiter measurement can precede or follow the Saturn measurement. But always, reference must be made to the relationships in the *birth* chart. In the example here, Jupiter is in excellent condition in the radix and is also sextile Saturn. Reference to the Ephemeris is essential to corroborate initial deductions. Knowing Jupiter's period and its relationship with Saturn's quickly gives great insight into a horoscope.

Mars requires two years to go once through the Zodiac. This means that in seven to seven-and-a-half years, Mars is in opposition to its birth position. Immediately, we see the relationship to Saturn's orbit; i.e., approximately when Saturn makes a quadrature aspect to its radical position, Mars is in opposition to its birth position. So, if both Mars and Saturn square a body in the birth chart, this situation will be accentuated somehow every seven to seven-and-a-half years. Secondly, we see that Mars and Saturn are in conjunction usually once every two years. It is invaluable to mark these conjunctions in a multi-year or "century" Ephemeris of monthly planet positions. When these conjunctions fall upon an important point in the horoscope or in significant aspect to a point, it may represent a significant inroad toward analysis. And, as we have seen in the examples on pages 173-174, knowing these transit phenomena helps us use Astrology quickly and adroitly "away from the office."

Speedreading Aspects:
This book assumes that the horoscope can be drawn accurately by the reader and that he can read aspects. There are slow and fast methods to deduce aspects. The following little chart is the basis for the fastest and easiest way.

	Cardinal	Fixed	Mutable
Fire	♈	♌	♐
Air	♎	♒	♊
Water	♋	♏	♓
Earth	♑	♉	♍

- The Signs within the same elemental family are in 120-degree trine aspect one to another: Aries-Leo-Sagittarius; Libra-Aquarius-Gemini; Cancer-Scorpio-Pisces; Capricorn-Taurus-Virgo. If we have the Sun in 10 Aries, any planet in Leo or Sagittarius at ten degrees will be in trine with the Sun. The eye spots a ten degree indication somewhere and checks the Sign: if the Sign is of the same family as the Sun Sign, there is a trine. Of course, especially for the Sun, we would look for the planet from three degrees to seventeen degrees in Leo or Sagittarius, allowing for the *orb* of the aspect, the margin of exactness.

- The Signs within the same mode—Cardinal, Fixed, or Mutable—regardless of elemental family, are in ninety-degree square or 180-degree opposition one to another. Aries to Libra, the opposite Sign: opposition; Aries to Cancer or to Capricorn: square. Cancer to Capricorn, the opposite Sign: opposition; Cancer to Libra or Aries: square, etc. If Mars were in 10 Capricorn, any planet in Aries or Libra at 10 degrees would be square. The eye spots a ten-degree position somewhere and checks the Sign: if the Sign is of the same *family* as the Sign holding the planet Mars, there is a *trine;* if of the same *mode,* in another Cardinal Sign in this case, there is a *square* (or opposition, if the Sign is the opposite one). Of course, for the planets, we would look for another planet from seven degrees to thirteen degrees, allowing for the narrower orb for planetary aspects, the margin of exactness.

- Sextiles, sixty-degree aspects, are read two Signs ahead or behind the planet concerned. Be careful not to skip over intercepted Signs!

- The Quincunx, 150 degrees, is one Sign back from the opposition within the same degree margin of the planet concerned; the Semi-square, forty-five degrees, is one Sign plus fifteen degrees added to the degree number of the planet concerned. (This book does not involve these aspects in examples, although in thorough analysis they are recorded as aspects corroborative of major aspects and measurements.)

Classic Patterns

The *Grand Trine* occurs when there is a planet in each of the three Signs of the same elemental family and when these planets are each 120 degrees from one another: Uranus in 13 Taurus trined by the Sun in 13 Virgo, which is trine to Jupiter in 17 Capricorn, which is trine to Uranus. These three planets are in trine to each other in the three Signs of the Earth family.

The Grand Trine forms a closed circuit. The meanings of the bodies involved in relation to the Houses flow into one another extremely easily. The energies follow this line of least resistance, like a cue ball on a three-sided table, bouncing continuously off one side, to another, to another, and back again. Click-click-click. A groove is worn on the playing surface. *The meaning of the elemental family, in this case Earth, dominates the significance of the whole.*

The Grand Trine in Earth Signs. The earth Signs are "down-to-earth." Capricorn is administrative, Taurus is planning and steadfastness, Virgo is detailed attention to tasks. Together in a closed circuit, there would be a stress on practicality and, always in the Grand Trine, *self-sufficiency.*

The Uranus-Sun-Jupiter example on page 133 suggests precisely these characteristics. The native is totally self-contained in her critical energies (Sun in Virgo) and has recurrent fantasies (Sun conjunct Neptune), which are rooted in the home (Sun-Neptune on the IVth cusp) and projected to the public and the husband (Jupiter in the VIIth); they embody the native's hopes and wishes and the love she expects (Uranus intercepted in the XIth) as reward for her ego (back to the Sun). *The Grand*

Trine tends to isolate energies and the part of the identity dependent upon these energies.

The Grand Trine in Water Signs. The emphasis here is emotional. Cancer is the well of emotionalism and mood; Scorpio is the deepest probe to the spirit's mysteries, on sexual, emotional, and religio-philosophical levels; Pisces is the absorbing blender. Together, in a closed circuit, there would be a grand stress on emotional self-containment; negatively: the "spoiled-brat" syndrome.

In the example on page 93, Mercury is just above the horizon in 11 Cancer (an emotionally sensitive person who plunges into deep moods through his own mental process) in trine with Jupiter in Scorpio in the Vth (he had deep thoughts about his emotional creativity, had even tried to become a minister) and in trine with Saturn in Pisces in the IXth (his ambition's direction and way are hard to distill, are emotionally oriented, perhaps in dual directions, and the process causes the mind to start over again with new emotional programs). This self-containment causes the emotions to demand their *own* circuit. The native is a performing artist and, learning of this Grand Trine circuit, at first tossed it off as artistic temperament!

The Grand Trine in Fire Signs. The Fire Signs are heated up. Aries is the fiery leader, blazing a path for the ego; Leo is the ruler through the light of the identity; and Sagittarius is the thrust of ideas and intellect, value judgment. Together, in a closed circuit, there is an inspirational self-sufficiency. The stress is upon the fire of the ego's particular Sun-Sign fuel.

In the example on page 186, the native has her Ascendant's ruler, Mercury, retrograde in Leo in the IIIrd. She has a counterpoint always within the communication of her ego. Mercury is trine to retrograde Saturn in Sagittarius in the VIth: her ambition is lofty and righteous, her opinions *must* be important in her working situation (and they will probably not be easily understood because of the privacy of this closed circuit and the retrogradation, the counterpoint). Saturn is trine to Uranus and Jupiter in Aries in the XIth: the inspirational circuitry is linked to expansive hopes and wishes about love to be received, the ideal, and bounces back to Mercury for refocus and more mental fuel.

The Grand Trine in Air Signs. Here is intellectual self-sufficiency. Libra's personality and social balance is emphasized extremely by the social uniqueness and mental acuity of Aquarius and is continuously making swift adjustments and rationalizations through Gemini. This Grand Trine is often a closed circuit used for *mental defense* against some threat to identity balance and self-esteem. It can also be found with identities, so self-contained intellectually, that they literally finish other people's sentences for them!—or they may stay silent, constantly repeating inwardly a construct of their minds.

The young woman whose horoscope appears on page 196 has had many years of difficulty with her mother (Sun opposed to Uranus from the IVth to the IXth-Xth; Moon in the VIIIth, ruler of the Xth). Her upset and tension have kept her personality's form and her thinking about it under wraps. Her energy potential (Mars) keeps things in balance but is locked away in the XIIth, giving more tension and frustration to the ego (squared by the Sun). This trine from the Moon to Mars carries on to the trine to Mercury-Jupiter in the IVth, echoing by rulership the problems of the Moon's Sign, the XIIth which holds Saturn, retrograde and in Virgo, and the Sagittarian IIIrd, communications, siblings, mental ability. The opposition between Pluto and the Ascendant ruler Venus, and the rising Neptune further mute the personality's thrust, playing into the hands of the subdued Capricorn. The native learned much from her horoscope and has chosen to begin teaching art and music—at

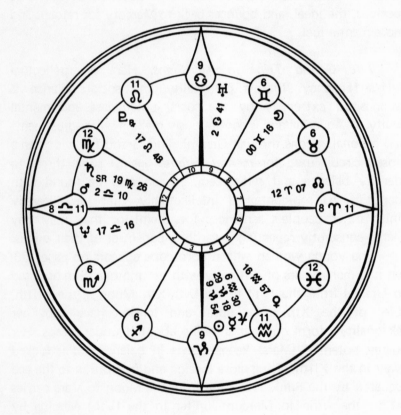

which she is quite accomplished—as a means to break the closed circuit and speak to the world.

Overall, the Grand Trine confines the possibilities of experience. There is extreme attention to the elemental family involved: inspiration and drive, emotions and sensitivity, practicality and sufficiency, thought and social communication. It is difficult for the identity to take on embellishing or modifying dimensions through experience, through relationships.

Often, one of the bodies involved in the "smooth" Grand Trine makes a "hard" square or opposition aspect to some other body. Then there is a potential way out of the closed circuit—and the way in.

In the Earth Grand Trine example on page 193, the Sun-Neptune conjunction was squared by Mars in the VIth, ruler of the XIth: if the native put her efficient, critical, administrative skills to work *for her husband's plan* and not for her own individuality's recognition, the circuit would solve many family problems and free the woman's individuality considerably.

In the Water Grand Trine, page 198, the woman has Jupiter in Scorpio in the IIIrd trined by Venus in Pisces in the VIIth, trine Pluto in Cancer in the XIth. This emotional self-containment was an enormous burden in the marriage. The woman could simply say, "I resent my kids!" Saturn, ruler of the Vth, was in conjunction with the Sun in the VIth, opposed by the Moon in the XIIth. The personality was extremely restricted in this complex chart. Yet there could be a way out. Jupiter in the Trine in the IIIrd *squared* the Full Moon axis. Deep altruistic communication with her husband about the marriage and her part in it might free the personality. Instead, the native went inward, pressed by extraordinary circumstance in the environment (transits: Mars-Saturn conjunct Midheaven, opposed by Neptune on the IVth, squaring the radical Saturn), and justified her emotional circuit through religious rationale

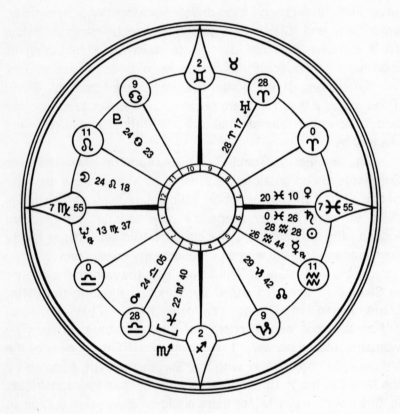

(Jupiter in Scorpio in the Trine), leaving things up to God, as if to say, "I am what I am." The marriage dissolved, but the break stirred the circuitry. She began to seek more deeply from others and undertook psychotherapy.

In the Fire Grand Trine example on page 194, the Saturn was squared by Venus in Virgo. This,though still difficult, might be a way out: to focus her social antennae (Venus) upon elders, wiser people, mentally gleaning *their* inspiration, understanding them, and then working to feel what others feel. —The Venus in Virgo position easily suggests someone who can talk about emotions without feeling them.

In the Air Grand Trine example on page 195, the education outlet will give the young woman a new audience and voice to redeem her self-esteem. In another example: Edgar Bergen, the ventriloquist, found his way out through an alter-ego, Charlie McCarthy. Here, Pluto's position in the Trine focused its public projection through entertainment, through a square from Venus in Pisces in the IInd.

The Grand Trine is a construction seen immediately, practically on the first look at the horoscope. It is a commanding figure when it appears and an extremely reliable guide to further analytical steps.

The T Cross or T Square is another powerful classic planetary arrangement. It is formed when a body makes a square to two other bodies in opposition; a third body squares the opposition axis formed by the other two. This arrangement is depicted as a cross with the headpiece missing. It is a highly dynamic configuration. —The T Cross is "discharged" into the zone where the headpiece would be if the formation were a perfect cross: for example, on page 69, the native has the Sun and Mars in 24 and 28 Scorpio, respectively, in the IVth, opposed by the Moon in 26 Taurus in the Xth, both squaring

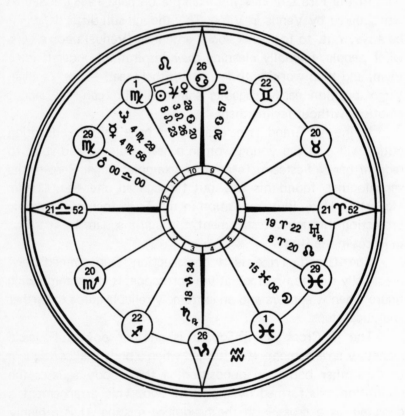

Neptune at 3 Virgo in the Ist (over the Sign line but within orb). The discharge here would be into the House opposite Neptune, into the missing headpiece zone, the VIIth. The life energy and personality form are charged with camouflage and suppression. The sexual overtones are high. The native is a homosexual trying to create a professional personality for himself, but he continuously gets taken in through involvements on a sexual level and his own self-delusion about his personal projection. Aquarius is on the VIIth, the discharge House: the public image is often in turmoil, appears eccentric at times; partnerships fail.

In the example on page 122, the woman has the Sun in 19 Virgo in the XIIth, opposing Saturn in 19 Pisces, retrograde in the VIth; both are squared by Jupiter in 16 Sagittarius in the IIIrd. Immediately one could expect sickness through the Sun in the XIIth exactly opposing Saturn in the VIth: trouble with the bowels (Virgo), the feet (Pisces), eczema (Saturn), and fertility (Saturn rules part of "unusual" Aquarius on the Vth). The Virgo can have much to do with pets, also linked with the VIth House. This tension Cross could also indicate such a detail as a black (Saturn) cat (VIth; female client!?) that died during childhood! All of these observations were corroborated. The discharge here would be into the IXth House (opposite Jupiter), foreign countries, higher philosophies, husband's communication: led by the husband's job the family lived abroad for several years. The wife found herself, a use for her talents, and became an active leader of many worthwhile community projects. New philosophies of life presented themselves to her, sicknesses abated, and her husband came to grips with an important life-theme in his communication goals. The "T" Cross discharge was managed superbly.

The example on page 200 has Pluto in 20 Cancer in the IXth, opposed by retrograde Saturn in 18 Capricorn in the IIIrd, both squaring retrograde Uranus in 19 Aries in the VIth: again one could expect sudden health debility, while traveling or in a

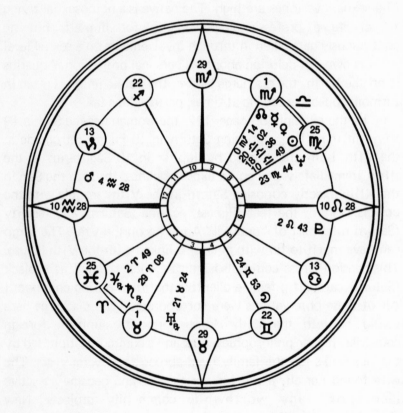

foreign country (Uranus in the VIth, Pluto in the IXth, Saturn in the IIIrd), perhaps in the knees (Saturn in his own Sign, Capricorn). The native did suffer rheumatoid arthritis in the knees. He traveled constantly and, with much discomfort, overwork, and absence from home, he felt many restrictions upon his personal life development (discharge into XII).

Another example, that on page 202, has Pluto in 2 Leo in the VIth opposed by Mars in 4 Aquarius in the XIIth, both squared by retrograde Saturn in 29 Aries (across the line but still within orb) in the IInd. With a Libra Sun intercepted in the VIIIth, sextile Pluto (ruler of the Xth) and trine Mars, ruler of Aries intercepted in the IInd, this T Cross showed the native's veiled personality, energetically involved with institutional service to many people (Mars in XII, Aquarius Ascendant and Pluto) making money, but defensive about his ambition. The horoscope spoke clearly to this astrologer about some kind of secret service. Corroboration was avoided by the client. The discharge would be into the IXth House: the native was employed abroad and was unable to describe his work.

The speedreading techniques discussed in this chapter can be mastered without a pencil! In a very short time, measurements can be approximated to establish several vital keys to the horoscope, to the core of the identity. The T Cross and Grand Trine are observations closest to real depth analysis since they involve several bodies and Houses. Practice of these techniques improves observation and speed of synthesis greatly. In a very short time, deductions can be made that save time, increase efficiency, give meaning to networks of aspects, and establish a developmental structure within time.

The astrologer is an observer. He must practice observation to the extent that another sense is developed, a sense he can trust in the responsibility of his service, in the challenge of his art.

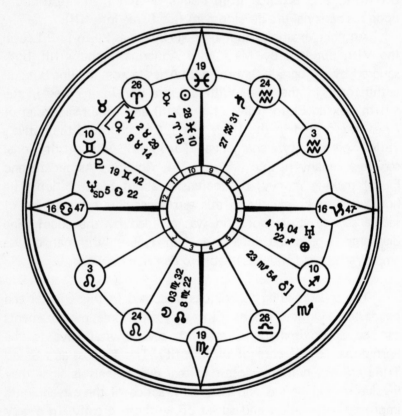

5
Three Special Cases

Albert Speer, Hitler's architect:
the builder and destiny

Albert Speer, whose chart appears on the facing page, was Hitler's architect, building with Hitler the plans for a colossal Berlin to be the center of a new ideological world, a monument to the new era that was to be Germany's. During the war struggle to assert this ideology, to end one era to begin another, Speer was given the key post of armaments minister and, in fact, became second only to Hitler as a power on the home front. Speer's intellect and technical genius finally perceived the futility of the dream, the waste of the land, the madness of the leader, and he plotted to assassinate his benefactor. The plot failed and, in Hitler's last moments before taking his own life, the two men stood together in the awareness of identity, destiny, and lost dreams.

Speer was the only Nazi leader to admit guilt at the Nuremberg trials. He was sentenced to twenty years in Spandau prison. During his imprisonment, Speer wrote his memoirs, published in English in 1970 (London: Weidenfield & Nicolson): *Albert Speer—Inside the Third Reich.*

In the first pages of the book, Speer reveals that he was born at noon in Mannheim, Germany (49 N - 9 E; Standard Time Meridian at 15 E, *no* Daylight Saving Time), on 19 March 1905.

The book is an extraordinary emotional experience. Speer has been criticized for his martyr-like stand—Was this a highly evolved identity speaking from the very core of a Piscean endowment? Speer has been lauded for his sincerity in tactical reversal to end the war—Was this the high-level triumph of his ambition projected to humanity, restricted earlier by the closed circuit of an artistically inspired, enormously practical (to the point of genius) Grand Trine in the Earth family? —Was Speer's endeavor, compressed into the few years that tore at the fabric of history, the fulfillment of a lofty destiny? Were his movingly human memoirs a way for us to see an architect working to reshape time, yet still subject to the Saturn that is time itself?

Inside the Third Reich offers so much to us for astrological study. The brief analysis that follows concentrates upon the eighteen years that include his work within Hitler's movement. Chiefly, only major progressions and transits are used, emphasizing events and reactions within time's environmental press. Every deduction is accompanied by a page number in parenthesis: these numbers index the page in his book where the occurrence or reaction is recorded.

At first glance, we see Saturn in Aquarius: ambition seeks a social projection for unique service, opportunity, and endorsement. Uranus will be important as ruler (with Saturn) of Aquarius. In the IXth House, Saturn will take on a high minded dimension, an international scope for ambition's expression. The Moon, symbol of the personality's form, is moving away from, but is still within orb of, an opposition to Saturn: the ambition axis had "straight-line," direct awareness contact with the core of the personality (the Moon rules the Cancer Ascendant). Moon square or opposing Saturn is a powerful aspect of expansion and determination. It is a T Cross with Mars, creating extraordinary tension toward fulfillment, discharged into the XIth, hopes, dreams.

The Sun is in Pisces near the Midheaven. The life energy could expect ascendancy professionally, perhaps in two or more roles (Pisces, a double-bodied Sign). The Sun trines Mars in Scorpio in the Vth: the life energy would be vital and deeply stirred emotionally, resulting in much creativity.

The Moon, Uranus, and the Venus-Jupiter conjunction form a Grand Trine in the Earth family: the personality and ambition are linked in a closed circuit of grand practical self-sufficiency. Venus-Neptune in Taurus (Venus ruling Taurus) suggests the aesthetic dimension of the work construct. Venus also rules the Libra Vth: further indication of artistic creativity. Venus is exalted in the Sun Sign Pisces, connecting its dimensions with the life energy and the Midheaven, the profession. The predominant Water (emotion) emphasis in the horoscope (Ascendant, Neptune, Sun, and Midheaven in Water Signs) focuses upon this artistic projection strongly as the mode of ambition's unique service on an international scale.

Neptune rising in Cancer is opposed by Uranus in Capricorn in the VIth (an angle of the Grand Trine): the ruling planet of Pisces, stationary-direct, links direct, imaginative, fantasized vision with the unique service genius involved in the Grand Trine circuit of endeavor. At the same time, there could be peculiar physical debility with the knees (Capricorn) and/or the stomach (Cancer), and a peculiar restriction upon the very genius of vision that might build the life and profession to a scale demanding grand acclaim. One motive could be substituted for another.

Pluto is the lure to the masses and is here in departing square from the Sun. The tension might be the lure of masses distracting life's concentration from the *personal* vision to be realized through the profession. This aspect could correspond to a duality of life application, registering as a restriction of the personal fulfillment of individual creativity (Pluto in the XIIth, co-ruler of Scorpio in the Vth).

Mercury rules Pluto's Sign of tenancy, Gemini. It is in Aries in the Xth. The fired mentality soars in a professional orbit, serving swiftly and ingeniously the demands of fantastic imagination, creativity, and work capacity. Mercury is linked with Neptune and Uranus in a T Cross in Cardinal Signs. The discharge House would be the IVth: the searing mental application in service to vision and ingenious work capacity causes tension in the home, is involved with a whirlpool in the homeland.

We note quickly in the Ephemeris that Mercury takes on retrograde motion at twenty-six years, as Saturn will be returning to its birth position. Here might be a turn of mind, the introduction of counterpoint, as ambition gains new focus and definite direction, perhaps fulfilling the duality promised by the Piscean Midheaven and Sun, and the square to Pluto in Gemini in the XIIth.

The rapport measurement Sun-trine-Uranus measures to thirty-seven, 1942, perhaps the finest time of Speer's life and professional work accomplishment.

The rapport measurement bringing the Sun to a square to the birth Saturn from 27 Taurus is sixty-one to sixty-two years, when Saturn will have returned a second time to its birth positon. Here we could expect a separation, a grand break, a reward from ambition's tension with the life energy; and, at the same time, the fulfillment of a life's dream, as Saturn would come in conjunction with the Sun. Speer was released from prison in October 1966, at sixty-one.

Uranus is a vital key in this horoscope. Its position figures prominently in both Grand Trine and T Cross. Uranus is the particular genius of this identity, at work with vision's service to ambition through world applications. Uranus and Neptune in radical opposition become important as transit energies in Speer's life.

Though we still lack definitive research and application of the "fixed" stars and constellations in astrological analysis, we should be aware always of their presences. Often, the inexplicable is illuminated by reference to them, and eventually a modern application of these classical positions may evolve. Still, it is remarkable how, if a horoscope has significant star involvement, it will have *many* such attachments. It seems to be often an either-or phenomenon: either the fixed stars are indicated many times or hardly at all. What can this mean? Is there some extra dimension working within the identity, infinitely too complex for us to understand, anticipate, manage? Is this phenomenon an index of real fate? It is a fascinating backdrop for Albert Speer's horoscope: *ten* fixed stars are involved, almost exactly—no wide orbs tolerated, only measuring conjunctions!

Scheat is conjunct the Sun; Algenib with Mercury; Sharaton and Hamal with Jupiter and Venus; Bellatrix with Pluto; Dirah with Neptune; Wasat and Propus with the Ascendant; Denebola with the Imum Coeli, the IVth cusp; and Agena with Mars. The enormously dramatized star of evil, Algol, at 25 Taurus, is squared by Saturn and opposed by Mars.

Another obscure dimension is the analysis of eclipses, beginning with the New Moon *preceding* birth. The number of eclipses involved significantly with the angles, planets, and lights in Speer's horoscope is so many that recording them in hopes of making order and seeking meaning became hopeless for this astrologer. In the first few years of life, seven eclipses of the Sun occurred in sharp relationship to the birth Moon, Uranus, Sun, Saturn, Mars, and Ascendant. In the years of activity concentrated upon here, there are some seventeen lunation phenomena that make seemingly important contact with birth positions. The New Moon *before* birth took place in 16 Pisces. There was an eclipse of the Sun and it occurred almost conjunct the Midheaven-to-be and square the birth position of Pluto. Are these indications of an eclipse of life energy and personal projection by the lure of some kind of karmic service, sacrifice, or fantastic vision projected to massed populations in world history?

The horoscope shows an identity of enormous scope. Its development has been embraced by time and absorbed by history.

Pluto transited Speer's Ascendant at the same time that Mercury took on retrograde motion. It would have been a time of deep personality transformation, an envelopment of the personality by the lure of the masses, perhaps becoming part of something revolutionary, sustained by a mental counterpoint, a new theme for the intellect, a turn of mind. The time was 1927 through 1931 when Speer was twenty-two to twenty-six: the wandering quadrant of Saturn's orbit, returning to the renewed focus of its return. It was at this time that the young architect saw the emergence of Hitler, climaxing with his becoming Member Number 474,481 in the NSDAP, Nazional Sozialistische Deutsche Arbeiterpartei, the Nazi Party, in January 1931.

Speer writes how the masses "determined the theme," how in a party rally "the personal unhappiness caused by the breakdown of the economy was replaced by a frenzy that demanded victims. And Hitler and Goebbels threw them the victims. By lashing out at their opponents and villifying the Jews they gave expression and direction to fierce, primal passions. —It was an utterly undramatic decision (joining the party). Then and ever afterward I scarcely felt myself to be a member of a political party. I was not choosing the NSDAP, but becoming a follower of Hitler, whose magnetic force had reached out to me the first time I saw him and had not, thereafter, released me." The "sight of discipline in a time of chaos, the impression of energy in an atmosphere of universal hopelessness" won Speer's allegiance (page 17).

The relationship between Speer's horoscope and Hitler's are many and strong: Hitler's Sun in 1 Taurus is conjunct Speer's Jupiter in the Grand Trine, trine to Speer's very important Uranus. Hitler was more than just an amateur architect himself. He made full sketches of projected buildings. Architecture consumed his attention in the early days of his rise. Hitler's well-known Mars-Venus conjunction in 17 Taurus is sextile Speer's Midheaven and Ascendant: Hitler's passion for the architecture of his rise, literally and figuratively, bound itself to Speer's professional and personal thrusts for fulfillment. Hitler's Pluto in 5 Gemini was sextile to Speer's Mercury, freeing the architect's mind with the projection to the masses, to world domination. This was further reinforced by Hitler's Midheaven trine to Speer's Mercury: the two architects merged in the building of dreams. And further· Hitler's north Node, conjunct Speer's Ascendant. Hitler's Neptune in 1 Gemini squared Speer's Moon in his Grand Trine: here was the tension with Hitler's fantasy, at first beguiling Speer with opportunity and then directing his energies to armament management and a position in the architecture of war, a camouflage of artistic fantasy.

When Saturn made its first return to its birth position, new direction for ambition was dramatically established. Speer became Hitler's chief architect, formally received a uniform, and began close personal work with the Leader. The precocious appointment, afforded by Speer's efficiency, style, and speed in creating plans for minor party buildings, gave outlet to Speer's enormous ambition and creativity: "My position as Hitler's architect had soon become indispensable to me. Not yet thirty, I saw before me the most exciting prospects an architect can dream of," wrote Speer in his chapter entitled, "My Catalyst" (pages 32 and 49). His promotion came two months before his twenty-ninth birthday.

Saturn came to a conjunction with Speer's Sun, a time of dream-fulfillment through his creative expression, in tune with grand collective goals, in the spring and winter of 1937. He won the Grand Prix at the Paris World Fair and earned from Hitler the "Great Assignment" for futuristic Berlin (pages 67 and 76). At the same time as this powerful transit, Speer experienced the progressed Full Moon, suggesting a time of seeing the light, in his Vth and XIth Houses of artistic expression and dreams; Uranus was in transit conjunct the Jupiter-Venus point; the progressed Sun had just entered Taurus, approaching conjunction with Jupiter and trine with Uranus. (There was in transit in June a New-Moon eclipse conjunct the radix Pluto, and in November a Full-Moon eclipse opposing the radical Mars in the Vth).

Speer became "enlightened" by the annexation of Austria and the devastation of synagogues in Berlin, when Saturn transited his Mercury, often correlated with a humanitarian wisdom, gravity, and ambition, bringing momentary anchor and perspective to the intellect (pages 109 and 111). Yet, the ambition and fired mind were still led by Hitler's hold: "I accepted what had happened rather indifferently. Some phrases of Hitler's, to the effect that he had not wanted these excesses, contributed to this attitude . . . what crossed my mind at the time: dismay over the deviation from the image I wanted to have of Hitler . . . but Hitler's hatred for the Jews seemed to me so much a matter of course that I gave it no serious thought. I felt myself to be Hitler's architect. Political events did not concern me. My job was merely to provide impressive backdrops for such events. And this view was reinforced daily." The closed circuit of the Grand Trine is dramatically evident here. And when Saturn conjoined Speer's Mercury it was trine Hitler's Midheaven and sextile his Pluto.

Speer's thirty-seventh year in 1942 was the time of the Russian front. And Speer was assigned to military constructions. Neptune transited in opposition to Speer's Sun and his life's vision was dramatically, strangely, fantastically altered: his return to Berlin from the hard winter in Russia via Rastenburg in East

Prussia was delayed in Rastenburg by conferences with Hitler and deep fatigue. He gave up his seat on the plane that was to carry him to Berlin. The plane crashed. "From that moment on my whole world changed" (pages 189 through 193). Did the architect feel a plan of fate? Was it rationalization, self-deception? After a talk with Hitler on that day, 8 February 1942: "That night our dreams were transformed into realities; we had once again worked ourselves up to a hallucinatory optimism." (Neptune opposed the Sun; Uranus and Saturn opposed Mars; Mars was conjunct Venus; Jupiter was approaching Pluto.)

When Saturn and Mars joined in conjunction transit with the radical Pluto in the XIIth, Speer's life was filled with intrigues, concerns about armaments (Pluto), and the masses of people involved. He felt lost and constricted in the expansion of the war. On 2 September 1943, Speer became Reich Minister of Armaments and War Production, surrounded by the intrigues of the inner circle. "Among friends I always called Bormann 'the man with the hedge clippers.' For he was forever using all his energy, cunning and brutality to prevent anyone from rising above a certain level. From then on, Bormann devoted his full capacities to reducing my power. After October, 1943, the Gauleiters formed a front against me. Before another year had passed, things became so difficult that I often wanted to give up and resign my post. . . . This (the industrial apparatus) was so much my own creation that my fall would have meant the end of it and thus have endangered the war effort" (pages 250 through 261, 275, *277,* 284). Saturn and Mars conjoined Pluto early in 1944, in the XIIth House of secret enemies.

Neptune in transit left the opposition to the Sun and made the square to Uranus in Capricorn in the VIth. The sudden sickness and knee problems that we could expect from the birth configuration, the Neptune-Uranus opposition, XII-VI, took place in December, 1943, and January, 1944. Speer was hospitalized and developed further complications as transiting Mars and Uranus were with transiting Saturn in the XIIth House: respiratory and arm troubles (Gemini). "For twenty days, I lay on my back, my leg immovable in a plaster cast, and had plenty of time to brood over my resentment and disappointments. A few hours after I was allowed to stand again, I felt violent pains in my back and chest. The blood in my sputum suggested a pulmonary embolism. . . . My condition remained distinctly critical . . . the doctors prepared my wife for the worst. But in contrast to this pessimism, I myself was feeling a remarkable euphoria. . . . Hovering between living and dying, I had a sense of well-being such as I had only rarely experienced" (page 331).

In the spring of 1944, upon his leaving the hospital, an incurable cardiac defect remained with him. Neptune's suggestion of strange feelings, alterations of opinions, and a new beginning (transit of the IVth House) continued: "My enemies were using lies and intrigues to eliminate me once and for all" (page 334).

Saturn squared the Sun, approaching the conjunction with Neptune. Tensions were mounting; new feelings were taking hold; an emotional era was ending. Self-deception (radical Neptune in the XIIth), secret enemies, and personal restrictions were taking their toll: "I did not query him, I did not query Himmler, I did not query Hitler, I did not speak with personal friends. I did not investigate—for I did not want to know what was happening there (Auschwitz). . . . During those few seconds, while Hanke was warning me, the whole responsibility had become a reality again. Those seconds were uppermost in my mind when I stated to the international court at the Nuremberg Trial that as an important member of the leadership of the Reich, I had to share the total responsibility for all that happened. For from that moment on, I was inescapably contaminated morally; from fear of discovering something which might have made me turn from my course, I had closed my eyes. This deliberate blindness outweighs whatever good I may have done or tried to do in the last period of the war . . ." (page 376).

Saturn came to the conjunction with the radical Neptune in the XIIth in August, 1944 (the New Moon opposed Saturn and squared Mars), and in February, 1945. Here would be a further focus of the breakdown in feeling, the awareness of responsibilities (Saturn). The structure of the Reich and the structure of the identity were collapsing. First transit: "On 30 August 1944, I informed the heads of my departments of my intention to make the Gauleiters (city heads) responsible for armaments production. I was going to capitulate. . . . I was driven to this because I no longer had any support behind me" (page 397). Second transit, February, 1945: "That night I came to the decision to eliminate Hitler. My preparations, to be sure, went no further than the initial stages and therefore have a touch of the ridiculous about them. But at the same time they are evidence of the nature of the regime and of the deformations in the character of its actors. To this day, I shudder at the thought of what that regime had led me to—I who had once wanted nothing more than to be Hitler's master builder" (page 429).

Saturn made a station upon the radical Neptune and assumed direct motion in April, 1945, and came to Speer's Ascendant in July. In April, *Jupiter* was conjunct the IVth, the end of the matter, a twelve-year period. Speer visited Hitler in his Berlin bunker in April: "Trembling, the prematurely aged man stood before me for the last time; the man to whom I had dedicated my life twelve years before. I was both moved and confused. For his part, he showed no emotion when we confronted one another. His words were as cold as his hand . . . For a moment I lost my composure, said something about coming back . . . I was dismissed . . . I was leaving the ruins of my building (the Chancellery, visited after leaving Hitler's bunker), and of the most significant years of my life" (page 485). With the announcement of Hitler's death on May 1, "the spell was broken, the magic extinguished. What remained were images of graveyards, of shattered cities, of millions of mourners, of concentration camps..." Two weeks later, staggered by the revelations of the crimes in the concentration camps, Speer wrote to the chairman of the ministerial cabinet: " 'The previous leadership of the German nation bears a collective guilt for the fate that now hangs over the German people. Each member of that leadership must personally assume his responsibility in such a way that the guilt which might otherwise descend upon the German people is expiated.' —With that, there began a segment of my life which has not ended to this day" (pages 488-489).

As Saturn completed transit of the Ascendant in July, the New Moon showed an eclipse of the Sun conjunct the Cancer Ascendant as well. Imprisoned and on trial, Speer suffered intense stomach pains (page 518). His identity, his individual genius, his intellectual efficiency, his work as architect of dreams and war stood before the peoples of the world. Uranus transited conjunct Pluto in the XIIth House.

In the spring of 1953, Speer in prison decided to write his memoirs when Uranus came to his Ascendant and Neptune was about to enter the Vth House of creativity (page 525). He finished the first draft of the book in December, 1954, as Uranus trined the Sun and Mars conjoined Saturn. Here was the identity finally working on the highest level of Saturn's call; the wisdom born out of the tragic struggles with responsibility, the creativity freed to redeem the individuality.

Speer was released from prison in October, 1966: Saturn had just touched his Sun, after its second return; a new dream was fulfilled; a new way was found for his special projection of ambition in unique service. He had his book with which to inform the world of an artist's role in a world crisis. Pluto was in conjunction with the IVth cusp, a new beginning with the world.

There was a progressed Full Moon, a seeing of the light. Thirty years before, he had become the chief architect and donned the uniform of another man's dream. Speer's artistic thrust was given dual directions, his vision was altered. At sixty-one, he had a new uniform, a new meeting with the people of the world, a new vision of life and destiny. The identity, whole again, assumed new life in the service to memories.

A businessman
a life divided, suicide or death

The circumstances concerning the case represented by the horoscope on page 218 were intense and tragic. The family was well-known. The husband was an important businessman with large public responsibilities. He traveled constantly and worked endlessly. Many times during the marriage, lonely and understandably suspicious, the wife had contemplated divorce. Husband and wife had not shared love for several years. Yet, a social image of gaiety and hospitality was maintained. The children were none the wiser. The husband claimed impotence to the wife. The wife bore her fears in silence.

The husband's horoscope shows three major structures: Mercury rising in Capricorn is trine to the Saturn-Jupiter conjunction in the VIIIth. The native's mind and skill with languages were superb. His business image was that of the administrative, efficient Capricorn in every way. His ambition manifested itself in hard work and the mastery of details; through his work he hoped somehow to prove his worth and find himself. A meeting with the man was a formidable experience, a meeting with a kind of ideal business power (Mercury conjunct the Capricorn Sun). He seemed a businessman's glamorous dream.

The second structure is the triple conjunction of Uranus, Mars and Venus in Pisces in the IInd, trine to Pluto on the cusp of the VIIth; a double-bodied Gemini on the Vth. This is an

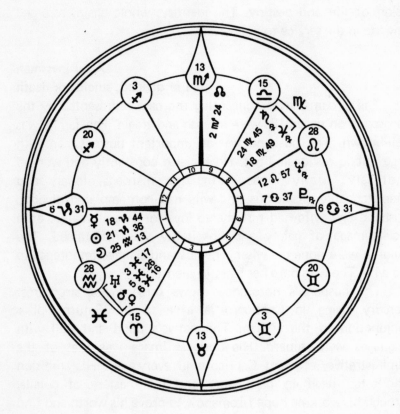

extraordinary sex profile: enormously intense, individualistic attention to the sensual, mysteriously (Pluto) linked to his needs from the public, his position in marriage, his finding himself through his profession (Pluto and Mars ruling the Scorpio Xth). There was little doubt that the man was *not* impotent, that there was subterfuge at work throughout his whole personality in relation to his wife and public image.

The third structure is the opposition between the Moon and Neptune, Neptune in the VIIth. Here was the "screen," between his business and sexual lives; the unique deception of his wife, also her self-deception in showing a public image of a happy marriage. The levels of his life were kept apart, held together by the fantasy and deception of his personality in relation to the home and the wife (Moon rules the Cancer VIIth). The excellent Mercury is the only body with a positive link above the horizon. Mercury and Saturn are in mutual reception, further reinforcing the fine business mind. Mercury rules Gemini on the Vth and VIth, and the plural affairs of this man were invariably with women he met in his work situation (also Scorpio on the Xth, links through Mars and Pluto to the sex structure).

Finance was deeply involved here (the Uranus-Mars-Venus conjunction in the IInd). Resources were lavished upon others secretly, emotionally; perhaps accompanied by mismanagement in business affairs (Aquarius on the IInd).

The wife was at a loss and, finally, after humiliating confrontations and discoveries, sued for divorce. The husband's progressed Sun opposes his progressed Jupiter, still retrograde, at 14 Virgo, suggesting legal difficulties, separations, limitations (ruler of the XIIth), even confinement. Progressed Uranus is exactly conjunct the radical Venus, inflaming the passions and financial situation, as well as the home (Venus rules Taurus on the IVth). The converse Midheaven is conjunct Saturn in the VIIIth.

The Moon is in progressed parallel with Neptune: epic

deception; Saturn is parallel Mars: the clash of ambition and passion. A positive sign is the progressed Sun's trine to the Midheaven, suggesting job honor, promotion.

The suit for divorce was presented as the husband received a grand promotion to a new position in a foreign country. The clash between lives was critical.

Neptune is also the planet of theatricality. The personality here certainly played two roles. The husband once told his wife that he couldn't talk about his trips from home because he was on "secret missions" for the goverment! (Pluto rules Scorpio on the Xth: secret profession, government.) Neptune suggests continual fantasizing by the personality, manifested in unique forms (Moon in Aquarius).

In *Astrology 30 Years Research,* Doris Chase Doane reports findings that suicide indications are a "Mars afflicted and a planet in the twelfth house, or the ruler of the twelfth house heavily afflicted. Progressed: an aspect to the ruler of the twelfth house at the same time there are severe Rallying Forces." This horoscope fits those conditions: Mars is "afflicted" by Uranus, and Saturn "afflicts" Jupiter, ruler of the XIIth. Radical and progressed Jupiter are opposed by the Sun in progression; the progressed Mars is four degrees from the square to the radical Mercury.

This astrologer received a call for help from the wife: the husband had threatened suicide many times in his life and again, in this moment of crisis, was making it extraordinarily clear that he intended to go through with it. At stake were the family's honor, the divorce and insurance settlements, and of course the love that once had been shared, the memories that had been growth.

The crisis occurred as a Mars-Saturn transit conjunction fell upon the wife's Ascendant and squared the husband's Uranus-Mars-Venus conjunction from his Vth. Neptune was in opposition to these transits and, thus, was crossing the wife's VIIth cusp and squaring the husband's IInd House group from the XIth.

Transiting Mars and Venus were in conjunction, Venus turning retrograde, upon the husband's VIIth cusp. Jupiter was retrograde in transit over his Ascendant. His fortunes and loves seemed to be "going away" from him.

There is indication of another problem in the horoscope: alcoholism, involving Neptune, the Water Signs, and the intensification by Mars. The progressed Uranus conjunct Venus is still "in conjunction" with Mars in Pisces. Transiting Neptune is square this complex. Radical Neptune is opposed by the Moon; Pluto is in the Moon's Sign Cancer. The VIIIth House emphasis with regard to the rising Mercury, ruler of Virgo intercepted in the VIIIth, shows us an identity trying hard to find itself, working under some inferiority feelings (retrogradation), in some counterpoint to actual reality. Alcoholism as a further camouflage in the personality was a valid suspicion, corroborated by the wife.

With the increase of tension, another dimension developed that brought the situation to mountainous crisis: a national magazine of the highest repute published an article about the businessman's firm (progressed Sun opposed Jupiter), naming the native, mentioning his inclination to drink, and suggesting his mismanagement of the firm's responsibility and financial image. The husband was in a frantic bind. —The call from the wife was now, "Will he commit suicide? When might he do it?"

There is a fine little booklet entitled *Astrology in Relation to Mind and Character* by a "mental specialist," published by Health Research (Mokelumne Hill, California 95245). It is an old manuscript, written in England probably in the 1920s. It studies so clearly the positive and negative mental indications in the horoscope. In speaking of suicide, the author calls attention to the importance of Mercury, the VIth, IXth, and IIIrd Houses, and of course the XIIth. In this horoscope, the Mercury is very strong and is not under "attack." Venus, ruler of the higher mind IXth (Libra) *is* under attack, but Jupiter is transiting the Ascendant.

Two other cases I have had concerning the attempt and threat of suicide corroborated the "mental specialist's" observations. In one, the VIth House Mercury squared the opposition of Pluto in the IXth and Mars in the IIIrd. Scorpio was on the Ascendant, and the Mars squared the Sun, Saturn, Jupiter, and Uranus in the VIIth! The Moon was in the VIIIth. This young man made the attempt and volunteered himself for psychiatric care.

In the other case, a woman had Mercury retrograde conjunct the Sun, opposed by Neptune in the VIIIth. Mercury rules Gemini on the VIth and Virgo held Neptune. Venus ruling the IXth was in conjunction with Uranus. Saturn was squared by the Moon and Pluto.

The first case had extraordinary tension mentally. Even the speech was affected. In the second example, with the introduction of Neptune, the tension was all fantasized drama.

In the case of the businessman, the Mercury was healthy and *had always proved itself.* It was the drama of losing the personality's shield that was the threat.

Transits for the month of the crisis have already been described. The Moon would eventually transit the XIIth House and come to the Ascendant in the last three days of the month in question. The progressed Moon was at 13 Capricorn; a new freedom of personality might come when the progressed Moon conjoined the radical Mercury in five months, the time he was to take his trip culminating in his new position, far away from the troubles at home. The transiting Moon would trace the crucial times: the transit would oppose Pluto, the transiting Mars and Venus, and cross the Ascendant. I advised the family that the crucial time was the last three days of the month; that suicide was a dramatic ruse, and that the mind would prevail as long as the Capricorn dignity was protected in the proceedings of business and divorce; that he should find focus upon the promotion and planned trip, a new life, due with the progressed New Moon in a few years; and that, should death occur because of the press of the environment, it would be by liquid, probably accidental overdose of sedative and/or alcohol.

The native was found dead at the beginning of the time period mentioned. The discovery was dramatic: the mistress claiming "suicide," the family standing strong as honors and memories and finance were collapsing. The death made newspaper headlines. An autopsy was demanded. The native died with 3.24% alcohol in his blood and from a circulation collapse due to simultaneous ingestion of blood-pressure medicine.

This is a very sad case indeed. The identity was divided. The cross to bear for growth was severely heavy. The search for self was on a grand scale, even to changing citizenship. Not understanding the needs of ambition, the expectancies within relaitonships, the honesty demanded to set love free, the permission to exist that is divine creation, kept this man victim of himself. His family lives on with the hope that sometime in the past he had had moments when he saw in them some fulfillment, some peace, some reflection of his identity's potential. In three years, the wife's progressed Sun will join her radical Pluto and trine Saturn; a new, wise self will bloom.

Judy Garland:
the mind and nerves, creativity to exhaustion

The world loves Judy Garland . . . still. Her entire lifetime was given to the public through her gifts of communication and performing art. *The Wizard of Oz,* the *Spirit of Saint Louis,* her concerts in the world's major theatres, the recordings, the

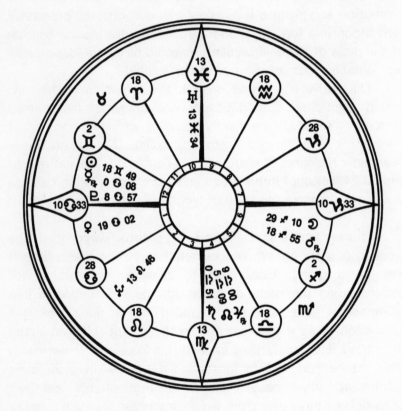

television appearances—a tremendous output embodying the genius of her creative communication enriched a generation. Her art lives on through a mysterious kind of eternal communication strength, and through the performing powers of her daughter, Liza Minelli.

The lives of great people, of people who fulfill their potentials, are never easy. There is always a struggle to set potential free, to maximize identity expression. Unusual growth emerges from unusual tension. Introspection and internal struggle give a vital truth to the external sharing. "Somewhere over the Rainbow," sung by Judy Garland as a simple, pure, and free little girl, remained her theme song in adult life, remained for the public the image of her spirit. The song's eternal significance to the development of every identity came to express poignantly the struggles within Judy Garland's personal life. Her struggles provided the very disciplines that produced communication and allowed her to share a search for fulfillment with millions.

Judy Garland, whose horoscope appears on page 224, was born on 10 June 1922 in Grand Rapids, Minnesota (47 N 20 - 93 W 29). According to Marc Edmund Jones's listing of 1000 birth times and planetary positions in *The Sabian Symbols in Astrology,* the time was 6:00 A.M. Grand Rapids is in the Central Time Zone.

The world knows that Judy Garland was tortured by nerves, depression, alcohol, drugs, and broken marriages. She never could keep her fortunes and, at the end of her life, had to borrow friends' homes for interviews.

The concentration upon the XIIth-VIth axis is clear. The ruling planet of the Gemini Sun, Mercury, is retrograde, with the Sun in the XIIth House, opposed by the Moon in the VIth. Judy Garland's Mercury and Moon command the entire personality (Moon rules the Ascendant). Her nervous system and personality form, her image, were constantly at odds, with a deep mental "counterpoint" providing inner fuel to the thrust (Sagittarius

Moon) of communication life-force (Gemini). There are no bodies in Earth Signs, and only Neptune is in a fixed Sign: an absence of practicality would deny anchor to the mercurial temperament awash in a dominant emotional emphasis (Mercury, Pluto, Ascendant, Venus, and Midheaven in Water Signs).

Mercury is square to Saturn in Libra: a nervous tension arising out of a struggle to achieve a balance between ambition and a secure home; a drive to communicate with the masses (Mercury conjunct Pluto; Pluto squared by Jupiter with Saturn in the IVth), a drive to attain rooted belonging. For a child star, the tensions and displacement involving the home would have been severely hard on the nerves and early formation of the identity. The T Cross (Saturn squaring the Mercury-Pluto opposition with the Moon) embodies a powerful demand upon the system, involving work, the home, and the entertainment industry that became her life and image structure. The T Cross discharges into the Xth House of profession, a whirlpool of anxiety, the intense work drive of artistic ambition.

The Sun exactly opposes the retrograde Mars, with the Moon in the VIth. The opposition promises precocity, enormous energy. She was "accident prone'" emotionally, mentally (Gemini-Sagittarius, mental Signs; sickness axis). The retrogradation of Mars would never change in the lifetime: the enormous energies would always go in before they went out; they would provide agitation and inflammation to the nerves and mental counterpoint, symbolized by Mercury retrograde, expanded by Jupiter retrograde.

The Sun-Mars opposition is squared by Uranus, alone in the Midheaven. This second T Cross introduces genius into the life drive of communication through the aesthetic profession, with international outlets. The intensification of the nervous structure is extreme. The discharge would be into the IIIrd/IVth House (with Leo, ruled by the Sun) of travel, communications, humor, contracts, and a search for a home (Virgo, ruled by

Mercury). Here were the accoutrements of her profession, the genius of her endowment, and the hope of her life.

Venus in Cancer, ruler of the creative Vth, was trine Uranus exactly conjunct the Midheaven. The Sun is sextile to Neptune, the planet of theatricality, ruler of the Midheaven. The indications in this horosocpe of a theatrical career are undeniable. Equally distinct are the indications of an identity that was champion of and victim to the profession and the creative gifts involved.

Theatrical charade was the only positive outlet for the nervous conflicts, the creative drive, the precocious and expansive ambition. Such stardom would take its toll upon the nervous system and emotions. Homes and marriages would be disrupted; *the* home would not be found easily, if at all.

Judy Garland attempted suicide on more than one occasion, according to the many news reports and stories about her life. The "affliction" to Mercury, ruler of the XIIth, in the XIIth, by Pluto, Saturn, and the Moon are key indications of the mental disruption that can lead to suicide. The Sun-Mars and Uranus T Cross would emphasize the unique identity tension and explosion further, involving the IXth, VIth, IIIrd, and XIIth. The Sun-Neptune sextile would support the theatricality of self-destruction, and Pluto's role in the complex would give the attempts public exposure, as if she were sacrificing herself to millions who shared her search. The same indications correspond to alcoholism and drugs: the mists camouflaging the garish colors of enormous internal tension and personal endeavor.

The horoscope is tortured with the need to be. Pluto rising, ruler of Scorpio in the Vth and so important in the configuration, takes the masses along with Judy Garland, to Oz, to St. Louis, to the concerts in London and New York. Millions shared her grief, her glory, her life and her death. The Sabian Symbols in Jones's book give the meaning "ultimate indestructibility of experience" to the nineteenth degree of

Gemini, Judy Garland's Sun. Indeed, her experience and gifts of life live for the world still. The communicator created grandly and was exhausted by the very act of creation.

Reflections Upon the Moon

The Moon "collects" the light, the influences." It is "the symbol of the personality's form," etc. So familiar. Do we picture the Moon chasing dimensions of the identity with some kind of net or sponge, capturing or absorbing potential reactions? The Sun is the energy of life. Is the Moon a room in an apartment house, close to the furnace, or far away, with heating problems, demanding better plumbing? Of course, each astrologer must come up with his own images, especially in teaching Astrology, in sharing the phenomenon of the Moon's registration in the horoscope.

The ancients had their complex spheres, circles within circles, their intricate harmonies. The circle is nature's form of completion. The awareness of the Moon's epicycle around the Earth not only simplified the deduction of the heavenly plan but worked hand in hand with heliocentric dogma to link the Lights to the energy source and identity form of Man. The energy was Sun-centered. In the extraordinary dynamism and order of Nature, the Moon related directly to both Sun *and* Earth; demonstratively, the Sun endows, the Moon distributes, gives further. The circles above interact with the lineality of man's awareness of his own time, his beginning and his end.

The Moon is correlated with a style of presentation of the identity's core energy. The style varies with the time of birth and the changing spatial relationship with the Sun during the lifetime. The drama of the variations has inspired language, art, and religion. Phenomena of fluids, temperament, fecundation, memory, and trends all find correspondence with the development of the Moon-Sun relationship. Identity finds reflection in the Moon.

Today, we *stand* upon the Moon. With billions of dollars, we seek to understand our earth's origin by studying the Moon. Is this not the dramatic coming to grips with the very tenets of Astrology? Has the relationship so observable between Earth and Moon been a tension of separation, a tension of rejoining? Is this why man projects a love and a romance to the Moon, in recognition of the relationship that *is* "natural" love? Is the allegory of relationship symbolized at every New Moon, with its new birth of light transmission; at every eclipse? We stand upon the Moon. Man turns himself inward in his quest for identity and outward to what might once have been part of him, by going to the relator, the related, the symbol of the form, the style of his identity.

Interpretation of the circle of the horoscope can be made on several levels: from spring through summer, to fall, winter, and spring again; from birth, to family, to relationship, acknowledgements, and death; from ego construction, to creative beginning, to public projection and recognition, and on to dissolution. The Moon finds its position somewhere within these interpretive circles. The position can be sharply defined, muted, lost, shadowed, energized, depressed, etc., in its meaning by virtue of its light, its illumination, and its relationship with the planets, all bound to the Sun for their existence and order.

We can look at the Moon as easily as we can look into a

mirror. To look at the Sun is blinding. The Moon reflects and translates the light of the Sun. We get the message. We see and recognize part of the light of life. By its nearness to us, the Moon is almost the same size as the Sun at its great distance. In the horoscope we see them both clearly.

The Moon in the Signs

The Sign in which the Moon is located reveals the *style* and *form* of life expression. The aspects made by the Moon at the moment of birth reveal the *energy values* and *structure* of the style and form. Consider the impossible: a horoscope without a Moon. The life would have no place to go, the light would not be reflected in any way, shape, or form. The Sign of the Moon is largely a focus of what man sees in other men, what others see in him. The Moon in a horoscope works hand in hand with the Ascendant to complete the *image* of identity, the specialization that is individuality, the gift of ourselves that we show, that we give to others. It is the symbol of psychological need.

Moon in Aries. The emotional temperament of the native with the Moon in Aries takes on emphasized ego dimension. Aries is the beginning of all, the spring, the thrust through the soil, the marshalling of forces to overcome obstacles; it is the style of growing, the thrust of effort, the heat of ascendancy. The Moon in Aries demands recognition. The temperament adjusts itself accordingly, i.e., in relation to the life-energy source, the Sun Sign, and the aspects. The mundane manifestation of the personality is the *House* position of the Moon.

Charles de Gaulle was a Sagittarian with Sun and Mercury conjunct the Midheaven: enormous, lofty accomplishment is suggested; the Sagittarian thrust of opinions and, here with Mercury, impressive skill in communicating ideals. This was an unusual man, indeed, with an Aquarian Ascendant, Jupiter and

Mars rising in conjunction in the Ist. Humanitarianism framed the entire arch of the life-energy promise. The Moon was in trine to the Sun and Mercury. It was in Aries: the ego was projected upon his France—his very name, de Gaulle! On a government level, the Aries influence becomes military; on a personal level, impatient demand.

The couple, whose horoscopes are briefly outlined on page 133, can be used as an example here again. The husband has an Aries Moon, without any aspect made in the horoscope. The Scorpio Sun is in the VIIIth, a deep life-energy source, a well, a furnace in the deepest cellar. The life cannot find attachment, personality form, recognition, ego definition easily. Here, the Aries Moon is stress without anchor, without direction. The frustration and problems within service of the creative energies, reflected in the sex profile, followed.

The artist Salvador Dali has the Moon in Aries conjunct the Midheaven, squaring Uranus. The Moon rules the Ascendant. The world regards Dali as a genius-eccentric. His clothing and living styles are totally individual; his painting style (Sun, Mercury, Venus, and Mars in Taurus) is an obscure esoteric statement, forcing its message through creative earth forms and natural architecture. His ego demands recognition, tyrannically, in other fields beyond his art. Remembering vividly the details of his previous existences, his personality lavishly calls for acknowledgement throughout time (Saturn in Aquarius in the VIIIth, square Mars-Mercury conjunction).

Moon in Taurus. Here, the Moon is said to be exalted. The structure of Taurus frames the personality's form well. The expressivity of the Moon gives meaning to the structure. The personality gains firmness. The reactions to life, *in* life, are careful, planned, and released judiciously, always with a strong respect for the aesthetic of individuality and the economy of sharing and value received. There is always a keen awareness of the identity's personal resources and worth.

Swedenborg, the transcendental mystic theologian, had the Moon and Uranus conjoined in Taurus. His uniqueness was his identity. He was totally self-contained in his translation of his visions into an earthly philosophy (Moon trined by Jupiter in Capricorn in the Ist). His "obstinacy" gave longevity to his beliefs and dignity to his being. He knew he was "right" in his perception of things as they were.

The opera singer, discussed on page 93, has the Moon in exact conjunction with Uranus in Taurus, opposing Jupiter in Scorpio, trining Neptune and Venus in the IIIrd. The Moon is related to *every* body and rules the Ascendant; his personality threatens always to run away with him, to flow away into many directions. His core of identity form is rooted in unique religious awareness. He patents inventions as well! His Water Grand Trine adds considerable emotional impress to the image.he builds. The aesthetic coherence suggested by the horoscope embraces all.

The art dealer, discussed on page 69, has the Taurus Moon in the Xth, in close opposition to his Scorpio Sun. The professional security of the identity is torn by other concerns in his life. He holds his views on aesthetics strongly, in protection of his worth, his self-esteem. The Sun rules the Leo Ascendant. His caution, care, planning, and economy are lessons learned the hard way, overcoming much opposition, with conscious determination and awareness of values.

Greta Garbo—so obscure, so rooted in her legend, her holding of her own philosophy, her aesthetic—has the Moon in Taurus in the XIIth, trine the Sun in Virgo in the Vth. The creative self is *determinedly* isolated. Her self-value is in high definition. She has communicated, and now she keeps to herself.

Moon in Gemini. Here the personality has something to say, seeks ways to communicate its messages. A very prominent banker (page 45) loves nothing more than to talk philosophy, about many topics, and to write his thoughts. A conductor with an Aries Sun and Virgo Ascendant (page 87) projects his personal leadership and detail management through a communicative personality form. A housewife fights for outlet: indecision and her environmental role work against the communication of her message; the result is gossip, too many things done halfway. The aloof leader of an international organization, Moon in Gemini in the XIIth, writes love poetry but will never discuss it.

Mussolini submitted to Hitler in order to speak to his own public (Moon in the VIIth in Gemini). Finding his own way was difficult: no oppositions in the horoscope, lack of focus; Moon losing light approaching the Sun.

Herbert von Karajan, the world famous conductor, has exploited his communication need through all kinds of orchestras, music forms, as well as through stage direction and total communication responsibility for festivals and epic productions (Moon conjunct Pluto in the VIIth, sextile to the Aries Sun on the Vth cusp).

Moon in Cancer. The Moon rules Cancer. Texts say that the Moon is at peace here, that the meditation dimensions of the emotions are emphasized; there is an openness to full emotional awareness. The identity is so ready to take in the light of others that a certain reactant passivity accompanies this position. The Moon in Cancer especially needs the stimulus, the definition of other planets. The openness to suggestion and stimulation is a prize, however, as well as a weakness in life. Relationships are built upon an exchange of light, and with the Moon in Cancer, the exchange is very dramatic: the Moon has such a capacity to take in and reflect further, as symbol of the public potential.

Isaac Newton's awareness of the world around him elevated him to a genius in history. His Moon in Cancer made a sextile to Mars: active energy was brought to deductions. Theodore Roosevelt had the Moon in Cancer in the public VIIth, opposing Mars rising in Capricorn. The rough-and-ready soldier, the man of the earth, was leavened by sensitivity and an emotional awareness of public welfare.

The housewife discussed on ' pages 129 and 36, with Sun-Mercury in Pisces opposed by Neptune in the VIIIth, has highly developed personal fantasies in search for her self. The Moon in late Cancer, nearing conjunction with the zero-degrees Leo Pluto, both in the Cancer VIIth, is square the Aries Saturn and the Aries Jupiter. Her imagination and sensitivities in the marriage defeat her effort to express herself. Defenses abound. The marriage dissolved into separation: the woman left to be alone with her feelings.

Moon in Leo. The Moon is in the Sun's Sign. The Sun is the source of the Moon's light. The emotions are given nobility, stature. The personality gains a royal integrity; it becomes hard to convince, difficult to sway. The native's interest and attention must be earned. A Moon in Leo strongly aspected can be at the root of a king complex. The manifestation need not be negative: the light somehow is "true." People recognize the kingly bearing, the earnestness of the emotions, the feelings, the reactions, the public perspective within the personality's form.

Oscar Wilde is a fine example: over-embellished in every phase of his expression; bearing himself like a monarch of letters. His supercilious wit was made acceptable, valuable, and memorable by the acute poise and sheer grandeur of his utterances (square to Mercury).

Disraeli, counsellor to a Queen and her era; a Taurus woman her Moon in Leo, ruling her household; a wife longing to be an actress and using her home as her stage—there are countless instances when the Moon in Leo leads a personality in its development to the challenge and reward of presidencies, directorships, and appointments.

The native with the Moon in Leo feels that recognition is owed to him, as if thinking, "I am my light." The native expects recognition, where the native with Moon in Aries goes after it. He communicates and dramatizes his position to tell it as it is. He structures his situations to show his importance. The light seeks an audience.

Moon in Virgo: As the Moon leaves the Sign of the Sun, the illumination is begun; work and endeavor follow. In Virgo, the Moon brings a keen practicality to the personality's efforts to shine. Knowledge is used for the task. Self-analysis and strong critical tendencies about life, others, and events are used to get under way. Order, neatness, and care trim the effort to efficiency.

J. P. Morgan, the great financier, had the Moon in Virgo on the second cusp. His great critical management of his personal resources channeled the life energies of his Aries Sun to grand accomplishment. The Moon opposed Uranus in the VIIth: his public projection was unique, philanthropic. The sextile with Saturn in Scorpio brought a formidable style to ambition and speculation.

A woman has an VIIIth House Sun in Libra, opposing Uranus in the IInd. Her husband died suddenly, shortly after her marriage. Her Moon in Virgo, conjoined with Venus and Neptune in the VIIth, corresponds to her personality's further development in the management of her husband's estate and business, and leaves her open to deception in this by others. She gives the utmost care to protecting herself in business and works hard to make her life grow out of the darkness of her short-lived marriage.

The husband of the housewife discussed on

pages 235, 129 and 36, has become married to his work. His Virgo Moon on the VIIth cusp has just left the Sun-Neptune-Jupiter conjunction in Virgo in the VIth.

Moon in Libra. This position brings a balance of judgment and an aesthetic to the personality's form. The aesthetic is not always as thorough or as structured as it is with the Moon in Taurus. In Libra, the ego dimension is easily accentuated; the feelings are easily and grandly opened to flattery. The balance of judgment, depending upon the aspects, can easily be upset.

Marie Antoinette, with a Cancer Ascendant, has her Moon square to Saturn. The Moon, Jupiter, Venus, and the Sun are in the Vth; Venus and the Sun, in Scorpio. Her personality's form, her style, her judgments, her sensuality served the tension of her practical ambition (Saturn in Capricorn). She managed her ego thrust and emotional style to build her ego.

Alfried Krupp von Bohlen und Halbach, heir to the munitions dynasty in Germany, had the Moon in the Xth squaring Mars and Uranus in Capricorn in the IInd. The Krupp empire sold arms *to both sides* in many, many wars throughout the world and throughout several hundred years. The neutrality in war was a phenomenon of finance. Alfried ruled in this spirit —Sun in Leo in the IXth— until imprisoned at Nuremberg. His Saturn squared Pluto on the VIIIth cusp.

Richard Leob (Leopold-Loeb Case) has the Moon in Libra squaring Uranus in the Vth and Neptune in the XIth. His Sun is conjunct Pluto in Gemini in the XIth.

Gloria Swanson has her Libra Moon conjunct the professional Midheaven, a Full-Moon birth, with the Sun in the IVth in Aries: a tremendous polarity of ego assertion and driving-yet-balanced aesthetic expression. This is reinforced by a sextile of the Moon to Uranus, trine to the Sun.

Moon in Scorpio. The Moon is in its fall in Scorpio. The

emotions are deepened and shadowed. The sensual arises. Pleasure needs and self-indulgence press. The mysteries of life lure the personality's attention inward for complicated adjustment. The form is strong, self-protecting, and private. The level of personality development is very important here to give a quality to the enormous personality potential.

The woman discussed on page 75 is deeply immersed in her emotional fulfillment. Her Moon-Jupiter retrograde conjunction in Scorpio is trine to retrograde Pluto in the Xth, in Cancer. She works professionally from her home to get some outlet for the feelings that preoccupy her. Her Aries Sun in the VIIth drives her to arrange her public contacts to gain emotional outlet. Mars retrograde squares the Pluto and bottles up much tension. When Pluto crossed the Libra Ascendant, opposing the Sun, the native was turned inside out in the tension to find the meaning of her feelings and fears.

A female teacher with the Sun in Gemini has her Scorpio Moon in the VIth, opposing Mercury in the XIIth and sextiling Jupiter in the Vth, with Neptune. She is an excellent teacher but, beyond her job, is preoccupied to the extreme with understanding, justifying, and gaining outlet for her thoughts about sex. Her nervous system, decision-making process, and creativity are bound up with her own acceptance of her deepest feelings.

Moon in Sagittarius. The higher-mind emphasis of Sagittarius lifts the emotions and gives them clarity. The fusion possible between emotional sensitivity and the call of the intellect can promise identities superb judgment and inspiration. There is a directness, an exuberance, a thrust, quickly registered, that is too swift for clutter, delay, or confusion. The personality's form takes flight—often with enthusiasm, good cheer, and brightness.

Friedrich Nietzsche, the German philosopher, had the Moon

rising in Sagittarius just below the Ascendant, in trine to Uranus in the IVth. The family and home situation of this thinker were extraordinarily debilitating (judging from the rest of the horoscope), but the public form of his intellect projected itself through history, undoubtedly in overcompensation for the home situation. His thoughts of the super-dimensions of identity and reincarnated intellect still influence existential thought (Moon ruler of the VIIIth).

T.E. Lawrence of Arabia became legend for daring, travels and existential philosophy. His Sagittarian Moon upon his VIIth cusp opposes the Neptune-Pluto conjunction in the XIIth. The Leo Sun and the conjunct Saturn and Mercury in IV are trined by the Moon. Lawrence was a soldier-philosopher of fortune, preoccupied with valorous death. Arabia is ruled by Sagittarius.

An inventor with Uranus rising has this ruling planet squared by the Moon in the Xth, conjunct its own North Node. The man is all ideas and professional application of them.

Moon in Capricorn. So many Astrology texts use the word "ruthless" for Moon in Capricorn. The Moon here is in its detriment, the Sign farthest from the Moon's own Sign Cancer. Sensitivity is diminished. The personality's motives express themselves without the cushion of emotional forethought. The form and style express naked motives and ambition. The judgment is cold, sharp, direct. The power to exploit opportunity is ever ready.

Robert Kennedy certainly received his share of criticism for supposed ruthlessness. His Moon in Capricorn in the Xth, sextile the Scorpio Sun in the VIIth, is conjunct Jupiter and squares Mars in the VIth.

Napoleon's Moon in Capricorn in the IVth opposed his Saturn in the Xth.

Hitler's Moon in Capricorn, conjunct Jupiter, was in his IIIrd House; Saturn was in Leo in the Xth.

Abraham Lincoln's Moon in Capricorn was also square to Mars in Libra. But his personality's edge was softened and dignified by two important dimensions: the sextile to Jupiter in Pisces in the IVth and the Saturn-Neptune conjunction upon the Sagittarian Ascendant. Privately, he suffered form deep depression and melancholy.

A powerful businessman has Moon in Capricorn (VIth House) in Grand Trine with Venus in Taurus and Neptune in Virgo. The Moon is square a retrograde Mars. The native works to excess at his job. The energies and drive from his Aries Sun are backed up. His practical self-sufficiency keeps him from sharing the workload. His individuality is intensified. He developed a heart condition.

Women with the Moon in Capricorn have a difficult time being graceful in their own bid for autonomy. They run the house and make the decisions. With the Moon in Capricorn in the Vth, a woman may exploit through sex motives other than emotional ones.

Moon in Aquarius. Here the personality takes on a humane projection. The welcome of the world to full expression is enjoyed. An instinct of community, of belonging, of world awareness is strong. The unique blends of the personality are expressed easily and often with unusual dimensions. The form is clear and intelligent; it involves education and unique arrangement of other talents.

The composer genius Richard Wagner had the Moon in Aquarius conjunct Mars in the Xth, sextile Neptune in the VIIth, square Uranus in Scorpio in the VIth. His unique projection of legend into a new music-drama form gave the world inspiration for new scope in opera presentation.

The housewife discussed on page 85, has only the Moon under the horizon, in Aquarius. In finding focus for her life and the expression of her Sun-Pluto in Leo in the Xth, she has immersed herself in history and the world-community through her removal to an ancient land. She has begun to study Astrology and religion.

President Nixon's Moon in Aquarius is in his VIth House of service, square to his Taurus Saturn in the IXth, sextile to Mars in the IVth, and trine to Pluto in the Xth!

Moon in Pisces. In Pisces, the emotions of the personality, the feelings, find sympathy. Don Quixote could have had the Sun in Sagittarius with the Moon in Pisces. The personality with the form suggested by the Moon in Pisces accepts the structure of the ideal. The receptivity is great. An aspect of definition and anchor should be hoped for to give definition and outlet to the identity's inner stores.

The Duke of Windsor had the Moon in Pisces in the Ist House in a Grand Trine (Water), with the Sun in Cancer in the Vth and Uranus in Scorpio in the IXth. He gave up his throne to follow his "ideal" romance with a foreign woman. His emotional construct demanded self-sufficiency.

Robert Louis Stevenson, Goethe, Shelley, Oscar Hammerstein, each with his Moon in Pisces, were men who gave form to feelings.

Naturally, the judgment of the Moon's reflection of life energy must be made in relation to the position of that life energy itself, the position of the Sun. In *Heaven Knows What,* Grant Lewi gives superb treatment to all the 144 possible combinations.

It is important here only to note several observations, for the reader's further thought and amplification.

Trines

When the Moon trines the Sun, the two lights are in Signs of the same elemental family, the same triplicity:

- Sun in Capricorn/Moon in Taurus: the personality structures management inclinations smoothly
- Sun in Capricorn/Moon in Virgo: the easy working out of the inclinations
- Sun in Taurus/Moon in Virgo: working out the structure
- Sun in Taurus/Moon in Capricorn: the personality administering the structure
- Sun in Virgo/Moon in Capricorn: dedication to work gets direct, sharp application in life management
- Sun in Virgo/Moon in Taurus: the work effort is well structured

The key meanings of each of the Signs work harmoniously together in trine relationships. In the *Fire* family, the drive and inspiration of Aries, the leadership of Leo, and the high-minded thrust of Sagittarius serve one another; in the *Water* family, the environmental sensitivity of Cancer, the depth and stature of Scorpio, and the receptivity of Pisces cooperate to fulfillment; in the *Air* family, the balance of observation and ego-attention of Libra, the uniqueness of Aquarius, and the swift adjustments and intelligence of Gemini work toegether impressivly.

Wide orbs of about fourteen degrees should be allowed. Observation of these relationships is an invaluable key at the first glimpse of the horoscope; ideas thus gained can be filled out during the next steps of analysis by distilling the Sign and House meanings in detail. *It is the Moon's registration in relation to the Sun that man sees in others, that others see in him. One can't alter the life energy, but one can shape the personality expression through the relatively swift progression of the Moon.*

Squares

When the Moon is in square to the Sun at the moment of birth, the two lights are in Signs of the same mode, Cardinal,

Fixed, or Mutable. If the square is very close, it can often mean that the native's family was uprooted or under tension at the time of birth. In all cases, *there is a tension between the life energy and the personality form given it,* involving the quality of the elemental family.

The thrust of one family struggles with the thrust of another. The Aries drive combats the Capricorn caution, in fields determined by the House placement and/or rulerships. The Aries drive can clash with the emotionality of the Cancer. The Capricorn caution and practicality can fight with the Libra blindspot, glamorous self-assurance. The Piscean receptivity can be lost with the vacillation of the Gemini, the soaring enthusiasm of the Sagittarian. The depth of the Scorpio stolidity has tension with Aquarian innovation and Leo extroversion, and so on.

Oppositions

These polarities of Sun and Moon can be difficult or challenging. The native must come to peace with himself with regard to the clarification of the form given his life energy.

- Sun in Capricorn/Moon in Cancer: practicality and emotions share the stage. The Moon can "show" the ambition sensitively, with perception, more "softly."
- Sun in Cancer/Moon in Capricorn: the personality's directness has less bite because the basic spark is tempered by emotional awareness.

Every astrologer must ponder these relationships to discover his own synthesis. *The Moon is the variable.* Its speed in progressions allows timely, conscious changes in personality presentation. Always, of course *the ideal is to serve the Sun best in relation to the native's level in life and the ambition forces of the horoscope.*

The Moon in the Houses

The personality form suggested by the Moon, in relation to its service to the Sun's life energy, manifests itself in the area of life defined by the House in which it is discovered. The aspects with the planets then add dimensions to the form and *establish the form's quality.* The House registration frames the synthesis in mundane experience.

Moon in the Ist House. The first House is the House of self: the ego thrust, the Ascendant, the appearance we present to others, the starting point toward maturity. The Moon, in its speed and sensitivity, invites change, adjustment, influence. In the first House, these changes, adjustments, and absorbed influences will affect the ego throughout life, especially at times of personal expansion or pressure. The native is inclined to mood-fluctuations, perhaps to delay. He can be very conscious of his own personal appearance and is very sensitive to public opinion.

Moon in the IInd House. Here the emphasis is on personal resources. The Sun-Moon relationship will express itself in earning money and promoting the identity through the meaning of the Moon in its complete synthesis. The receptivity of the Moon may admit the superficial here, the glittering but shallow. There is a certain charm to this position—the personality fluctuating and adjusting the form of its application of personal resources to suit public expectations, to establish self-worth.

Moon in the IIIrd House. The personality's form is in a mental House. There could be pronounced curiosity, memory ability (with an aspect from Saturn), a very keen awareness of communication modes. The personality takes on mental influences gladly. There may be humor, conversation ability. In these directions, based upon the Sun-Moon relationship and the aspects, the personality form works its best.

Moon in the IVth House. The Home, homeland, and mother are brought into very important focus. One author suggests a fondness for antiques associated with this position, and I have found this detail to be valid. The emotional bonds to the home permeate the personality. The condition of the homelife and its functional importance in the personality expression are shown through the aspects.

Moon in the Vth House. The creativity is accentuated within the personality's form. The Vth House is the House of the native's giving, his actual emotional, sexual expression. There is a note of publicity and public appeal linked with the Moon in this position.

Moon in the VIth House. The work situation is symbolically affected by the speed and changeability of the Moon. Numerous job changes can be expected. The changeability is an effort to find proper focus of service. Of course, under strong aspect here, the Moon registers the vulnerability to sickness in accordance with its Sign and the Signs involved with the aspecting planets.

Moon in the VIIth House. The Moon here accents its own suggestions of "public opinion." In the horoscope on page   , the native's Libra Moon showed her always in awareness of her social balance and public acceptance. When Uranus transited the Moon, the balance was altered, and a new dimension of her individuality rose in sharp relief.

Moon in the VIIIth House. The personality finds itself in self-doubt. The need for security is great, especially if the Moon is afflicted. The possibility of morbid concerns is strong. The interests seem to be narrowed. The VIIIth is the second of the VIIth: the personality's reaction to the partner's resources should be checked as a possible key to insecurity or loss of focus upon personal value. The possibility of jealousy should also be checked.

Moon in the IXth House. In the House of the higher mind, the Moon indicates inspiration. The personality may be so uplifted as to lose practical anchor, depending upon the Sun-Moon Sign relationship, of course. This position is the "dreamer" position.

Moon in the Xth House. Again, the Moon's public overtones are accentuated: the career, the awareness of the people served by the profession, public honor, reputation. The Moon here can shift the symbolism of the mother from the IVth to the Xth.

Moon in the XIth House. The native's security depends on his expectations of love and attention from others, his friends, his own particular brand of hopes and wishes. Often, with intervening interception, the Moon in the XIth House can be square to a planet in the IXth (usually a sextile prevails). In this case, the aspirations of the native would definitely be a key consideration for understanding his personality expression/frustration (see IXth House above).

Moon in the XIIth House. Here, the Moon is most restricted. There can be a veil over the personality expression, a separateness, an aloofness. The native may have some very particular sensitivity about himself or his background that easily becomes a personal restriction in the form of secrecy or fear of embarrassment. The moodiness can be enervating. At the same time, the public dimension of the Moon suggests fine personality projection within large organizations, hospitals, service agencies.

By no means, is the list above complete. It is only an indication of *the way of synthesis* and the great potential for personality diversity. Brief, practical synthesis, distilled by every astrologer for his own use, is the tool of adept, relevant analysis.

Throughout the charted cases in this book, one can see this elementary structure of synthesis vividly registered in the horoscope:

- In the horoscope on page 18, the Moon in Aquarius (with the Sun and Saturn) near the Midheaven certainly corresponds to the native's personality projection to the public, through a profession, uniquely (teacher-singer-cantor).

- In the horoscope on page 26, the Moon in Cancer conjunct Pluto in the Vth puts the emphasis upon the creativity for the public, which dominates the businessman-turned-artist. The Moon is in sextile to the Sun in Taurus: the aesthetic structure and financial emphasis (IInd House) are the base for the Moon's creative personality form.

- The horoscope on page 32 is touched upon again above (Moon in the VIIth). One can add that, with her Sun in Cancer in the IVth, squared (fourteen degrees) by the Moon, the tension was between her balanced public projection of personality and the demand of motherhood and care for the home, as we have already seen.

- In the horoscope on page 144, the Moon of this performer is in III in Sagittarius. He's a communicator.

His Sun is in Libra, sextile the Moon. His life force is for social balance and recognition of his aesthetic and ego.

- In the horoscope on page 148, the Piscean Moon, so open to suggestion, has given aesthetic, public, and professional form (in the Xth) to the life energy symbolized by Sun-Neptune in Virgo in the Vth.

- In the horoscope on page 152, the personality's form is in unique Aquarius in exact opposition with the Sun in the Xth. Honoration of the self has taken on highly unusual personality forms through sex.

- For Albert Speer, page 204, the capacity to work is the expression of the personality's form (reinforced so strongly by the Earth Grand Trine). The Sun's high elevation in Pisces in the Xth calls for public professions in the artistic field. The rapport measurement to the Full Moon is twenty-five to twenty-six degrees, when Speer joined the Nazi Party.

- In the case of the businessman, discussed on page 218, the Sun's position in Capricorn would offer the possibility of management and ambition. The registration of the Moon's personality form, in Aquarius, Moon opposing Neptune in the VIIth, deluded in unique ways the call of the life energy. Both lights together in the Ist House accent the ego concerns strongly.

- Judy Garland's Moon (page 224) is in the VIth—her personality was known for its tremendous work, service, and sickness—in Sagittarius, the higher-mind. The aspects here create a negative dynamism that brought professional success in projection but deep personal unfulfillment.

The manifestations of the Moon's meaning—in its Sign, in relationship with the Sun, in the Houses, and in aspect with the planets—are endless. So are the potentials of personality expression in a given identity. *The myriad possibilities are narrowed by the fact that the moment of birth, depicted in the horoscope, delineates one particular identity with its potentials built upon the base of the Sun, augmented by the relationship of the Moon with that Sun, and characterized by the planetary relationships to the base.*

Indeed, we do stand upon the Moon, every moment of our lives, every moment of our life time.

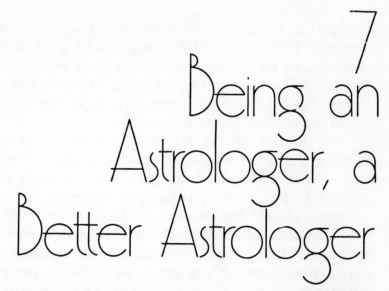

7
Being an Astrologer, a Better Astrologer

Astrology deals with the hopes, fears, dreams, and challenges of life; the potentials that are identity. It is the art of synthesis, discovering the themes of development within experience and time. In a very real sense, the astrologer is an artist. He is working with creations and the process of creation. He is close to the inexplicable fundamentals of cyclic life. He has an awesome responsibility as heir to a revered legacy. The astrologer is a lens through which the celestial immensity can be focused.

Every man senses at one level or another his lonely, tiny position within time, within the cosmos. In this space age, the individuals of the world are gaining a perspective on the infinite: science shows order beyond imagination; man is more clearly defined as an identity, but his total world and spiritual frame of reference are expanded beyond his mental or spiritual grasp. In his moments of introspection, man knows there is more to his existence than the workings of his ego. While man's arena expands out of sight, his will weakens in its potential to define his significance. The will becomes specialized, seeking to cut out distinct identity from vast panorama. With this discrepancy between ego and firmament, man senses or acknowledges fate.

His awe of his position in existence produces fear. Since Astrology professes a working knowledge of some of these mysteries, an interpretation of the drama in the heavens in relation to the drama on earth, Astrology is feared. Man fears that the free will he fights to assert will be completely overcome by learning of other existential dimensions.

At the core of the fear is the assumption of *causal* relationship between heavens and ego: "Do you mean to tell me that, if Mars and Venus team up on me, I'm gonna die or somethin'?" This typical kind of question accents the fear for the ego through loss of free will. This fear haunts the majority. It is the major factor that keeps people from coming to an astrologer. It is the factor that often *tempts the astrologer into over-explanation or over-selling Astrology to prove his Art-Science.*

Client expectation

Grant Lewi wrote, "Astrology is not something to believe in; it's something to know about." I have found this to be the very best first reply to the typical question, "Do you really believe in that stuff?" The question about causation is best handled by a kindly "of course not" or "Of course, the planets don't make you *do* things." These replies give respect to the questioner's feelings and give dignity to the astrologer. The questioner is usually stimulated further. His fear diminishes, and his *instinct to belong to the mysteries that are life* begins to reveal itself.

It is quite simple—and sometimes poetic—to explain that the phenomena observed in man's experience throughout history, in their relation to the movements in the heavens, have *correspondences,* not effects or causes. If the questioner has ever marvelled at an eclipse, he has shared the feelings men have had since man's beginning. He can appreciate that, in a world without electricity and air pollution, the drama in the heavens was much,

much brighter and compelling; that the bodies above were used to keep time and regulate crops; that with observation of nature and man, correspondences were seen between the movements above and natural and human developments below. The observations and their importance grew with time, and ever-developing intellect gave them meaning and, eventually, religious stature.

To explain much further puts the astrologer on show. He can't possibly give a speedy presentation of the interweavings of Astrology or its history. If the moment allows observations and corroborations about Sun Sign and/or Ascendant (pages 168 to 175), then perhaps the astrologer can make a dramatic point. If the opportunity is not reliable enough in relation to the astrologer's personal style and technique, the less said the better. Reserve and dignity about Astrology serve to protect its seriousness: an important and profitable distinction, in contrast with the "entertainment" periodicals and booklets that inflate Sun-Sign generalities monstrously out of proportion. The querent's instinct to belong is accompanied by an expectation of mystery, of esoteric knowledge from the astrologer.

By and large, the questions asked about Astrology are *valid.* And the astrologer gains greatly by actually agreeing with the statements made to him. The statements are usually correct; it is only the proper fuller explanation that is missing.

Often an astrologer is asked to give an example of Astrology at work, and here is a very real trap. The tendency is to give a highly dramatic example, read somewhere or from an actual case study. The highly dramatic example is given, a new client perhaps is gained, but then the client finds nothing so dramatic in his own horoscope. He may have expected a drama similar to the one offered in the example. Maybe the life of the client is going smoothly or quietly. Trying to match the drama of the example can prove demeaning and frustrating to both client and astrologer.

Hand in hand with *over-selling* is the danger of *over-promising*. Except in unusual cases where on-the-spot deductions lead the astrologer quickly to a potential answer, a promise of "seeing all" represents a dangerously empty hope to the questioner. "Can you tell me if my cancer operation will be successful?" Or the question I just received on the telephone forty minutes ago: "Everything is going wrong. Our dog broke his leg and our horse is lame. Should we shoot the horse? What's happening to us?" The question here really was not about the dog or the horse, or even about what actually was happening. The question was really "What time are we in, what are we going through on our way to development?" The Virgo woman, so fond of pets and affluent enough to have a horse, had a birth Sun square Mars. The Sun had progressed to an exact square with her radical Jupiter: a time when her natural "accident-prone" energies would be stirred up to excess, an excess in this case of self-embellishment, indulgence, and expansion. The horse had been bought within the year as the progressed aspect became exact. An astrologer might have advised against the excessive expenditure at that time (as her Saturn also approached her Ascendant), and channelled her resources toward calm preparation for the shift in life to come (in this case, through her husband). A little careful questioning showed that the whole household was stirred up in the process of change. Futures were at stake, new dreams. The purchase of the horse had been unsound and simply aggravated the larger situation. Recognizing this, feeling sorry for the horse and relieving its suffering would free attention and energy to the new goals and demands ahead.

Often a promise of help is interpreted too specifically by a client. Often the real counsel has little to do with the actual specific problem. There are those who want the concrete word of the astrologer to replace the weakness of their own will toward self-application. A promise by the astrologer is a very, very subtle thing, a suggestion of enormous value and lasting effect: the promise to discover and/or the promise from deduction.

In modern times, patience and peace are the two rarest virtues. The astrologer should first frame his client in a sense of time, as revealed in his life. Understanding the past helps to anticipate the future. By feeling his position in time, the client feels a correspondence with the heavenly bodies and sees the free-will decisions that have delineated his *level* in life. This is the promise of Astrology: to share the awareness and significance of time; the development of identity. The client's specific questions re-framed within this promise are invariably well answered. To promise otherwise or to promise insensitively *in order to prove Astrology* is to create expectations only God can fulfill.

The astrologer's ego

Let's face it. Analyzing a horoscope for a client is a performance! Both client and astrologer are tuned into the hour-or-so in which very important exchanges take place. Both identities are in communion, and money exchanges hands. The astrologer must focus all his creativity on his art; he must communicate significantly; he uses a great deal of energy. *His* whole identity is involved as well as the client's!

In the instant of meeting with the client, the astrologer makes judgments. He reacts subjectively—he has to—and converts his observations and feelings into objective deductions. He must contend with his instinctive liking for the client, his disliking, his pity, his envy, his sexual attraction, the age discrepancy, etc. He may be carrying several other horoscopes actively in his mind. He is concerned with his own home and work situations, his children, the book he may be writing, the party he will attend. *It is very difficult to be objective under the emotional challenge of horoscope analysis.*

The astrologer Zoltan Mason once told me that he keeps his

own horoscope on his desk for comparison with the horoscope of every client, to "see if I can be helpful," to see how *he* fits in with the identity of the client.

In my own personal situation, having a strong Capricorn Sun, Moon in Leo and being six-feet-ten inches tall with a deep voice, I easily can be over-authoritative. This can intimidate a client in his moment of sorrow or weakness; this can clash with a client in his moment of nervous drive or stubbornness. A partnership takes place during the astrologer-client meeting. It is a moment of tension that can bring out the traits, positive and negative, listed on page   . Careful preparation for this meeting of identities promises the best results.

If the astrologer's Saturn falls near the client's Ascendant, for example, the tendency will be for the astrologer to enforce his deductions upon the client's identity. The client will usually succumb, lose his free-will awareness, and sacrifice the strength and benefit of the dialogue. If there is attraction horoscopically or in feeling, there often is great value in acknowledging it, releasing the tension for one or both parties, and beginning dialogue with social ease and reinforcement of the client's identity. The Signs and House positions of the Saturns should be compared to establish direction and mode of the two ambitions. Saturn in Aries with its open and active defenses can exasperate the stolidity of Saturn in Capricorn, and vice versa.

With experience, of course, the astrologer grooms his objectivity and spares his emotional involvement. *Understanding subjective reaction invigorates deduction and definitely opens the door to intuition.*

Communication

Often within the pages of this book, the "first impression," the registration of the moment, is stressed. With experience and discipline, the first glimpse of identity can become extraordinarily valid. The identity exists in the person and in the horoscope. The human form transmits energies depicted in the horoscope.

We have seen groupings and progressions within a horoscope that can be measured and assimilated quickly. To learn to achieve a concrete first impression, and then to refine it, can save much work and time. Additionally, the mystical dimension of intuition can be awakened.

Intuition is a very precious guide. However, its occurrence is as unpredictable as snow on Christmas Eve: it can complete the picture perfectly but is not essential. *The cardinal rule is for the astrologer never to say anything he cannot see in the horoscope,* no matter how strong the intuition. Then, if intuition—that flash of awareness—and horoscopic discoveries coincide, we enjoy a gift.

The horoscope on page 258 is that of a client in Europe who applied for a job at many, many colleges in the United States. He wanted desperately to return home and teach. He had just married and was deeply depressed about where he would go. His transiting Saturn was very near his Midheaven and the radical Uranus (he had every reason to expect some achievement, some confirmation of his individual worth professionally). But his Sun was in the XIIth with Pluto, Mercury, and Mars, square the Uranus. As he explained his feelings of restriction, I received in a flash the thought that success was imminent for him—not just an acknowledgement of the Saturn transit, but a real glimpse of him successful, fulfilled, happy, productive, very soon in the United States. I felt the culmination of Saturn in terms of time. I knew that, in a month, transiting Saturn would join Uranus. I knew deeply he would be rewarded somehow!

But this transit would occur under difficult conditions, with the Uranus squared by the Sun and the other XIIth House bodies. These aspects would indicate tension and institutional

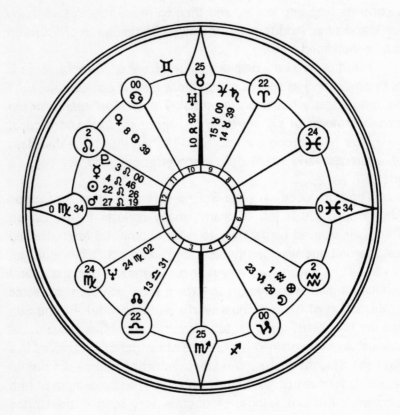

restriction. Academically, the Saturn transit conjunct Uranus would activate the square, hopefully positively. This "seen" evidence was not enough to give my strong intuition freedom to speak.

I checked the Ephemeris carefully, looking for corroboration. I found that, five weeks later, the transiting Sun would join the radical Jupiter in the IXth; Mars would transit over the Part of Fortune in Uranus' Sign Aquarius on the cusp of the "work" VIth; Mercury would make a station and assume direct motion trine to the radical Sun from the IXth; Saturn would be over the radical Uranus; and, finally, the transiting Moon (on a day when all these transits were as near partile together as possible, centering on the Mercury station) would pass over its North Node in the IInd. Here was every indication of illuminated fortunes in a foreign country; activated fortunes in relation to work and service; a message (Mercury) in harmony with life energy; an accentuation of individuality, ambition, and professional accomplishment; and the personality's form enjoying a bit of luck with its resources, money earned.

I felt that my intuition had confirmation and offered the client encouragement for positive news five weeks into the future, especially on one particular day. Two days before *the* day, he received a telephone call from a college in the midwest, requesting his services and arranging for his immediate flight there for an interview, on the day previously noted!

This case reflects the spark of intuition and the real science of Astrology working hand in hand—a grand embellishment. Some astrologers have a measure of clairvoyance. Each man must carefully distill his own particular gifts and refine his elements of style.

In the example above, the radical horoscope shows promise for teaching in foreign countries. There was no doubt. The intuition had to do with *time* and reinforcement of the birth-chart promise. Corroboration was found and the two worked dramatically together.

Intuition is a rare dimension. But the horoscope always speaks, even to the point of *defying subjective speculation.* An example: Mr. Mason analyzed my horoscope before I had any knowledge of Astrology. I barely could have been able to name all the Sun Signs. He looked up slowly from the chart and said, "Astrology. You can be an astrologer. I do not see it in you, but I see it in your horoscope." —Amen!

Elements of style

In an article about managing potentials in life, I wrote about style in personal expression. I suggested that style was "grace under pressure." This grace is a reliance on discipline that has become instinct. Fine singing in opera, for example, under the pressure of audience, lights, critics, career development, composer's demands, and colleagues, involves enormous discipline and poise. The fine singers in opera perform with a very discernible *disciplined abandon.* The mastery of technique and the confidence they learn in their craft and taste—their creative ethic—are their style. A golf pro teeing off under enormous pressures knows his craft and must *assume* its response to the demands of new situations.

Astrology presents great responsibilities, great pressure to the astrologer. He has worlds to learn: not just refinement of astrological techniques, but the philosophies involved with thought, religion, business, art, sex, politics, birth, death, medicine, psychology, anthropology, statistics, etc.,—even weather! The techniques of horoscope preparation and analysis approach the scientific. The communication to the client is the art form, the expression of sound deductions. The astrologer is the vessel for the knowledge, the lens of focus: he gives meaning to the substance of identity within time. One identity is communicated *through* another. The scientific disciplines become internalized; they become instinct and emerge through the astrologer, through elements of his grace and style.

Astrologers hear so much about ethics. In times past, when Astrology was practiced under pseudonyms, behind many closed doors, when jail sentences threatened, technique and ethics were certainly suspect, if ever easily observed. Today, there is much less suspicion, surely: Astrology is in the open, on the covers of leading magazines. The question is not the ethics of Astrology but the ethics of the astrolog*er,* the individual medium for the ageless wisdom.

Very much the same situation exists with doctors. "Is he a good doctor?" —"He's one of the best in New York!" How often we hear this. People give effusive personal endorsements of a doctor, without knowing anything about medicine and very little about other doctors. The treatment worked. The waiting time in the outer office was minimal. The personal manner of the doctor was calm, healing, bringing the patient back together. The personal quotient, the doctor's elements of style seem to determine his stature.

Conversely, a doctor's reputation or community profile can be diminished when the advice he has given is different from what the patient wanted to hear. How often this happens in Astrology practice!

Doctors recommend other doctors when the patient needs special treatment or is changing geographic area. They look into a directory and judge by educational background, age, perhaps address! The recommendation is made with very little actual awareness of the elements of style that are so important in the patient's judgment of services rendered. Of course, one doctor can judge another in actual practice, and this judgment would reach much further into the depth of knowledge and technique of practice than judgment by the patient.

Astrologers can judge other astrologers similarly. But how often do they go to other astrologers for assistance, for fresh insight, for self-comparison?

It is so easy to criticize. "The doctor says that the funny little pains in my husband's chest have nothing to do with the heart, that he's just nervous about our trip. But I know he's working too hard. It's his heart. The doctor doesn't know what he's talking about!" This is all too familiar. In the case of the astrologer: "He told me that my lame horse really is a secondary issue. He was sorry about it, but he says that I should give my attention and energy to these big changes coming up. Does he really know what he's talking about?"

When an astrologer is shown by a client the written work or told the spoken deductions of another astrologer previously visited by the client, he *can* make a judgment. I have seen some tragic situations: one woman was given a written horoscope as a gift. The "astrologer" knew nothing about the native. He inquired about nothing and wrote a fantastic, religiously fatalistic paper that was totally inscrutable to the client and me. I found myself tenderly apologizing for the work of this man, defending again and again the integrity of Astrology, trying to regain the trust of the client in Astrology and restore a definition of her own free will, her own integrity, her own identity.

This other "astrologer" had not studied the elements of his own personal style. He enforced a view upon an identity. He proselytized.

How do we communicate? How do we study the propriety and efficacy of our communication? How does our style *vary with different clients?* These questions are important guides to becoming a better astrologer. If we are much older than the client, it's harder to understand his viewpoint. If we are much younger, it's harder for us to gain respect for our deductions. *The horoscope is not absolute.* There is no cookbook that gives every recipe precisely to every taste. If there were, if everyone could learn to sing, everyone could do it! Astrologers dangerously oversell the scientific gounding of astrological measurements and deduction. This book emphasizes suggestions to speed deductions, to appreciate the wholeness of the identity before magnifying an internal specific. Where do we stop? *The answer is knowing where measurements and deductions stop and synthesis and communication begin; where relationship with client begins; where the "love" in the moment of rapport and awareness leads to an appreciation of identity and a position in time. The personal quotient of the astrologer's identity embellishes the scientific disciplines of his art. One must be as highly refined and polished as the other.* Working toward ease in this process is to develop style and create grace.

The relationship with the client is certainly like the relationship between doctor and patient. I once said to a doctor under dire circumstances, in appreciation of his superb attention and performance, that he made me want to become a doctor. He replied that this was the ultimate compliment. It symbolized the merging of identities, the sharing, the relationship that relieved a burden in life.

Because of the personal quotient, the identity of the astrologer, no two astrologers communicate in the same way. One may be incredibly skilled in deduction and weak, halting, or vague in personal communication, without grounding in applied living. Another may be extraordinarily glib in communication, shining in performance, but awkward or esoteric in deductions. Certain astrologers write beautifully about the meanings and philosophies of Astrology but have nothing to do with personal counselling. There are brilliant, senior astrologers who have lost the gift of communication; their books are inscrutable; a whole new language has evolved that defeats the communication between author and reader, between astrologer and client.

Formal education is essential to be a nuclear physicist. But formal education is not essential to be an astrologer. The techniques of chart construction and reading aspects are far too easy. It is with deductions and communication, synthesis and relationship, that the challenge to the astrologer's identity is made. Formal education helps mightily, of course, but there are many astrologers who have developed deep gifts, endowments of their own into a skill of communication that is formidable. Often, after a particularly successful client relationship, I am asked if my having a degree in psychology makes me a better astrologer (the client can't conceive that a horoscope can say so much!). In good humor, my reply simply turns the question around to "being an astrologer makes me a better psychologist!" I am *not* a psychologist, but the point here is that our *academic* skills enjoy Astrology as their extension. An astrologer who never went to college has found in Astrology an extension of his special identity. He may have to work harder to refine it and to expand it, but his integrity and value, his responsibility to this craft cannot be suspect through the dimension of education alone. It's what and how he communicates that is his measure.

It's curious to observe how many famous authors, in interviews, don't seem to talk very well. There are many great talkers who have to hire professional writers. Clients often criticize astrologers as being dull, obtuse, old-fashioned. These are valid criticisms in relation to the modern expectations of modern clients that should cause us to inspect our techniques of communication (bringing together). We must always work to improve our style, whatever it is, to polish it, make it flexible, and keep it up to date.

In the last four years, I have learned to speak, read, and write German. My goal was to be able eventually to do horoscopes in German. This is a formidable task. I realized I simply could not expect to communicate in the same style in German as I do in English. My personal style relies upon the aesthetic of special word combinations and images to make points, a kind of rhythm of narrative. For German, I had to simplify. In the beginning I would write out an outline of deductions in English, find the real essence of the thought, and come up with pithy, simple German sentences. Not only did this distillation process speed my German communication efficiency, but it improved my English style as well. I found that I could synthesize many horoscopes in three or four words. For example: a client worked "undercover" somehow. He wouldn't reveal his job to me. His life seemed to abound in the subtle control of others. He was always slightly suspended above relationships. After our long and profitable talk together, he asked for a pithy summation, something he could easily remember to trigger recall of our sharing. I said three words: "cultivate overt enthusiasm," and the relaxation and self-awareness of the biggest smile imaginable covered his face, and mine!

Few astrologers write out their deductions. I do, often, because I have clients in many countries and clients who are always travelling. It is an excellent way to bring order and refinement to deductions. A short summation written out can be a reference help in times ahead for the client, as well as a record for the astrologer's files. Writing even the smallest summary can help enormously to prepare the spoken presentation: the communication begins and knows where it is going.

Communication demands dialogue. Corroboration of deductions establishes level of reaction and development. To let the client speak is essential to bring deductions into living, practical focus. Often this is difficult: the client will maybe offer nothing. He wants some magic expectation proved by the astrologer, some out-of-the-blue deduction that will prove that Astrology *is* magical, and working for him! This is a difficult attitude. Sometimes a dramatic reading of details *is* needed, if the horoscope presents the opportunity, to stir the client out of his "show me" position.

For example, a client had Sun conjunct Pluto in Cancer

rising. His Mercury in Cancer was in the XIIth. His Moon and Uranus were in exact conjunction in the XIth, opposed by Jupiter in Scorpio in the Vth. Saturn was opposed by Neptune and Venus, IXth to IIIrd. Mars in Libra was square Sun-Pluto. Here was a deeply emotional native whose Grand Trine in Water (Mercury, Saturn, Jupiter) involved him tightly with his own emotional thoughts, restricting his relationships and feeding public upheavals in his life energy (Sun-Pluto). The potential for collusion was clear, the inclination to deception, all in an effort to secretly distill the way and direction of his ambition. When Saturn opposed the Sun and was entering the VIIIth, triggering the Sun-Mars square, the native would surely have had a low point in life, a time of frustration. Saturn ruled the public, wife, and partnerships of Capricorn on the VIIth. Immediately after this opposition to the Sun, Saturn squared the Moon-Uranus conjunction in the XIth, House of friends and the client's expectations from them. The Moon ruled the Ascendant and made an aspect with every body in the horoscope. Uranus ruled the VIIIth (partner's resources) where Saturn was in transit.

The client was standoffish (emotionally self-sufficient). He did corroborate that he had entered into a business partnership at that time. I suggested that there had been every temptation to *mismanage* wilfully his partner's funds. I communicated the suggestion dramatically, looking at the client sharply. He exploded with corroboration, saying that no one in the world knew that fact, that he had been so involved. The closed circuit was released, the client was strangely relieved concerning this moment long in the past, and the meeting of identities became extremely profitable.

Overall, the astrologer is caught in the struggle between free will and fate. It is the fear in the client; it is the dilemma for the astrologer. His phrases easily anthropomorphize the planets: Saturn brings *his* influence here and there, the Moon *enjoys* the

IIIrd House, *she* shines brightly on this or that, Venus and *her* beauty, Mars and *his* fire, etc. We are influenced by texts from many eras of superstition and literary style. We feel the drama so intensely, so animatedly. The "causal" explanation is all too easy and theatrical, but it does not do justice to the free will of the client and the profitable use of Astrology. Is not our objective to give strength and knowledge of the identity's worth, and its developmental progress through time? Is not our responsibility to build cognizance of free will, help with its focus and direction, bringing identity and hopes together in efficiency and renewed energy?

An astrologer performs a deep service. His scientific method allows disciplined deduction. His communication creates sharing. The revered legacy of Astrology inspires emotion and affords practicality. The identity is recognized, appreciated, focused, and guided through time.

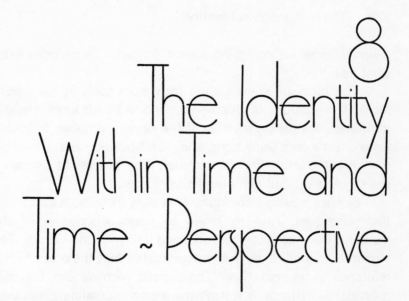

The Identity Within Time and Time ~ Perspective

8

Science is dedicated to touching the infinite scale of creation. Science describes the facts of existence, but it is for man *in* his existence within the infinite scale to interpret the awareness, the facts. That man has the ability to interpret, the access to meaning, is at one and the same time his glorification as a thinking, feeling incarnation and his millstone as a fearing, scrambling inconsequence. The knowing of life is a transcendental endowment and a humiliating burden. The identity in its awareness is face to face with God.

Man is. He is autonomous. His identity breathes itself to fulfillment in time. The organism absorbs the food of nature and the spirit of relationships. He seeks purpose, significance, and focus. At the dawn of the Aquarian Age, he is finding the God that lives within, the Godliness that is in man by the very act of his being created in the existential image of God. The reappearance of Christ—the man-part of the creating principle—in the "fulness of time" will be the symbolic fulfillment of the potentials of all creation. Autonomy will be given meaning through the realized relationship with God. As man waits, he is conscious of the tension between his creation-form and the divine scheme. He hopes, he dreams, he seeks, he struggles to be what he is.

The birth of science gives man more tools in his search. More information is discovered, and man deduces grander meanings. But the perspective of the world has grown infinitely faster than man's deductions, and man's position has come into even more clearly diminished relief. The process of discovery exalts man's will but diminishes his presence.

Science creates techniques. It creates techniques to support the techniques. And to relate to newer discoveries of the moment, man sacrifices his sustaining link with the eternal. The human autonomy is so highly accentuated that the present loses reference to eternal time. The present narrows and becomes specialized. Patience is lost. Peace seems impossible because of the urgency of self-fulfillment and identity definition in the present.

Yet, as man dies, he is said to *be* at peace. Leaving the present brings a virtue. Poets relate man's death to a sleep. Has he found something? Has his dream dome true? A baby is born, with long struggle and enormous energy, with incredible instincts and potential. Does he already have something? Does he have purpose? Why is the time of birth so very, very important? Why do births within families often astoundingly duplicate themselves in date, time, planetary configuration? The moment of birth is. It is the transition time to the challenge of the present. The identity is seen at a glance in the record of this moment. Time begins—*or is it continuing?* Is a greater awareness of the significance of birth a way for man to justify his inevitable death, to find a peace for his struggle, a focus of his autonomous identity?

In Matthew 17:9-10, it is written: "And as they came down from the mountain, Jesus charged them, saying, Tell the vision to no man, until the Son of man be risen again from the dead. . ." The word "again" is a key to illuminate our existential isolation.

Reincarnation is security. Reincarnation justifies death. The Seasons come; the Seasons go. We die to come again. We sleep to awaken refreshed. In every horoscope, we pay respect to this philosophic axiom every time we consider the IVth House: the end of the matter, the new beginning. The Imum Coeli is a point of beginning that, to exist, must be a point of ending.

We speak constantly of potentials. We accumulate enormous existence-energies in a lifetime. At death, where does the identity go? Indeed, the life lives on in memories, which are energies of considerable inspirational and active value. But everything in life, in nature, is resurrection. All of nature rejoices at birth. New life is salvation for the identity. It is in the birth, the moment of inspiration (the breathing in), that we have a refreshed perspective of the eternal. The present broadens, and we feel less the press of time. The endowment of free will *selects* this all-important moment for new beginning: during life or before it. The doctrine of Karma gives freedom of choice and the reason to be.

Experience is the structural necessity for Karma, for potentials, for will. Life as a circle (continuous flow) gains a radius of time (beginning and end). There is a circular unity to the cycles of nature. The Yin is the Yang, *because of* the Yang. A man is his mother because of her, his wife because of her. Man is God and God is man. These bonds are the unity of all potentialities. The circle is nature's sign of perfection; it is the Sign of the Sun with man within.

The astrologer is partner to the circle. He relates "circles" of heaven to the lines of time. He witnesses beginnings and ends, ends and beginnings, yet all within an eternal flow to some immense fulfillment. His service is to delineate perspective and give integrity, security, and value to the meanings of the present. Man works within his life, his curve-portion of a grander circle, to fill the arc with experience-figures that have meaning; he fills the arc to exhaust the space, to give meaning to the parabola. At death, the total form is not complete, though the momentary space has been defined.

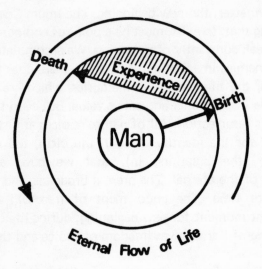

In the Nicomachean Ethics, Aristotle defines *kairos* as "the good in the category of time." It is the moment of time good for fulfillment of something. We read of kairos in Ecclesiastes. We feel the kairos when things go "right" in life. The kairos is Saturn's promise. Human greatness is the fulfillment of potentials within time. Discovering the kairos is the identity's quest for freedom.

Man's free will is his tension before God and his freedom within Karma. It involves him in the ambiguity of choice and decision. Guilt, shame, inferiority, compensation, transference all torment his trial. Is it any wonder that he often seeks an escape *from* this freedom? The kairos is elusive, the autonomy is bewildering. But reaffirmation of the circle can bring anchor; *renewed perspective translates time.*

The son of Saturn

Pluto was born of Kronos and Rhea. He was the brother of Zeus and Poseidon. Pluto came into consciousness of the world on 21 January 1930. When discovered, Pluto was in 19 Cancer, the Sign of "his father's" detriment. Mars was in 18 Capricorn, in opposition, in awareness aspect to Pluto's occurrence. Writers suggest that the successive discoveries of Uranus, Neptune, and Pluto in the eighteenth, nineteenth, and twentieth centuries, respectively, recognize harbingers of the times. Rudhyar observes that the period of Neptune is twice, and that of Pluto three times the length of the period of Uranus. This is unique. And I note that, at the time of Pluto's discovery, the Sun had just entered Aquarius. Has an age, an era really been announced?

Several suggestions have been offered for Pluto's meaning. Science makes the discovery, and man has the burden to give meaning. We are to divine the messenger's message. Research was intensive. We now have Pluto's Ephemeris back to the time of Christ. Inserting Pluto in the horoscopes of the celebrated in history corroborates many of the meanings suggested.

Pluto symbolizes the masses: its appearance in our century coincides with the largest population the world has ever known. *Pluto symbolizes upheaval and alteration of perspective:* its discovery coincided with the simultaneous rise of Nazism and world conflict. Pluto's entrance into Leo during 1938-40 accompanied the explosion of world war, the fall of governments and the slaughter of millions. Pluto has been given rulership of armaments and the atomic bomb (and the corroborations in Speer's horoscope are impressive). Pluto has just entered Libra in 1971 through 1972: law and order, human justice, is a world issue, while incomprehensible war still rages. The institution of marriage is being "modernized." The *raison d'etre* of the United Nations is being questioned: its new leader is an Austrian and its newest member is mainland China, both countries theoretically ruled by Libra.

For the individual, Pluto has meaning as well. Man's identity exists in a collectivity. Overpopulation threatens his very autonomy even further. He is a target of the massed media. He is one of many. —In each man is the capacity for the upheaval of change, the Pheonix's fall to rise again. He flees his freedom in revolt; he leaves his family, his job, his generation's ways, his country, his God. Pluto may mean for man *his capacity to turn himself inside out to find the God within, the creativity for full awareness of potential, the establishment of perspective.* Psychoanalysis, political dogma, nihilism; maturation, evolvement, metamorphosis.

Pluto was the king of the Underworld. Was he to marshal his hosts above the surface, to meet Mars in opposition, warring above the swell of change? Pluto reaches its perihelion (the nearest point to the Sun) in 1988 in Scorpio. Just before entering Scorpio, Pluto will be nearer the Sun than Neptune, and Rudhyar suggests the seeding of Neptunian ideals during this period will last until 2000. In 1989, Uranus, Neptune, and Saturn will come together early in Capricorn (upon this writer's Sun!), while sextile to Pluto. Will the full message have been heard?

Pluto may be the symbol of reincarnation. The death necessary for rebirth; the ashes of baptism. Are we not all children of God? Are we not to rise from the dead, again, after having seen the vision? Might Pluto in Scorpio correspond to knowledge of life and death fulfilled in man, to defeating sickness and healing the already dead, to discovering and understanding ancient mysteries?

Uranus rules the age. Its meaning is invention and individuality; the emphasis is upon identity. In the marvelous order above, Uranus spends seven years in each Sign and, after transiting four Signs (28 years), a new beginning is made in Saturn's architectural plan. Rudhyar points out how, in the not too distant future, man's lifespan will average eighty-four years, a complete revolution of Uranus around the Sun. Man in modern times is gaining time. His development accelerates and intensifies in the fulness of time.

Vision and Awareness

Martin Buber describes man's state not in terms of lost faith—of his insecurity—but as "the night of an expectation." He speaks of vision, "the Word of God," as the light of a falling star. Man is witness to the illumination. The light may vanish, no stone may be found, yet *he knows that it happened!* This is the awareness of being.

As we walk, we rise and fall. As we live, we change levels of achievement. All of us do. And the awareness of another is the awareness of sharing a common position in time. The whole is more tolerable with another; relationship eases autonomy.

The identity is constantly reaching out for relationship: through a glance, a conversation, an interest in another's well-bieing, fulfillment in another's growth, love. The relationship is communicated in an instant; one whole somehow finds another. The horoscopes of identities show their wholeness within time. In their corresponding drama, the planets act at many levels. Man in his growth easily misinterprets his role, gives an inferior performance, an incomplete interpretation. With time, his will gains technique and significance in the world. The immensity bears witness; Zeus speaks (Odyssey, Book I):

See, O Gods, how these Mortals complain of us, seeing in us the Source of all their evils, while it is they who by their deeds of rashness bring upon themselves the THINGS OUTSIDE THEIR FATE!"

Epilogue

How vital awareness is! With awareness keenly honed, we have the potential for sharp response. In many ways, awareness is the predisposition that "makes things happen": the highest levels of sensitivity prepare man and lead him to greater growth.

So often, when our technique in astrological analysis becomes frustrated, when we cannot solve the problem before us, it is because our awareness is dulled somehow, because we are not wholly ourselves. We try to make what we know about planets in certain Signs in specific relationships mean something in relation to the picture of identity before us. We try to apply literal meanings to unique situations.

It is interesting that our *sensory* systems have no trouble at all reacting to meetings, measuring stimuli of a new nature. We record observations in a flash. We register a vast spectrum of feelings about every "picture" we see in life. Why can we not free these feelings, this awareness, in experiencing new horoscopes as well?

Too, too often, we want behavioral phenomena explained in terms of aspects and planetary positions entirely. When we meet someone on the street, we do not immediately note the color of

277

his eyes, the placement of his nose, the balance of his ears on the sides of his head. We somehow get an impression, a whole "form" of awareness, and *then,* in our awareness of the encounter, we begin to punctuate this impression with salient features of its physical composition. So too can we react to a horoscope: we can see the life energy, the show of self, the mode and area of best application; we can see the general timing of development. Just the pattern alone can tell much about "zonal development" within the life-flow.

Additionally, awareness tells us that the owner of the horoscope and we the astrologers live *at the same time.* We share a moment in time. Keenly alert, we must know the operation and value of ambition and sexual energy, the creative forces within the present. The astrologer's field of reference includes the modern time *and* the client. The relationship between the astrologer and the client polarizes all there is between them.

A "cook-book" recipe for the horoscope simply does not give dignity to the meeting of identities within time. Theoretically, if a recipe fits the behavior, much is accomplished to prove the "science" of Astrology. But, operationally, is that important? When a client visits an astrologer, he is not touring a laboratory. In many, many ways he is coming to church: he is coming to hear words of selfhood and meanings of time. The sharing between astrologer and client, then, is one of *combined* awareness: it is not an experiment; it is a celebration.

Indeed, technical observations about positions, aspects, and cycles are the structure of Astrology. But its flesh and blood are the moment of meeting, sharing, and productive awareness. The structure constantly changes, as does the substance, in pace with the times.

The focus is upon the astrologer and *his* wholeness even more than it is upon the horoscope. How full he must be! How open to expansion and growth! In his work, he embraces eons of time and mysterious truths. In his relationship with the client, he takes into his hands and self the hopes, fears, and drama of another's identity. The astrologer must be prepared for the skill of his work and the responsibility of his service. He must be able to shift approach, levels of empathy, scope of interpretation, style of delivery. He must be aware of many fields and forms of life.

These thoughts are focused in one mighty sentence by Dane Rudhyar, a light of Astrology for forty years, in his *Astrology of Personality:*

> *No astrologer—and as well no psychoanalyst—can interpret a life and destiny at a level higher than that at which he himself functions.*

Rudhyar's words are a benediction for the astrologer. They motivate the sensitive astrologer to a fulness of function in the fulness of time. To show one astrologer seeking this path, I have offered this book.

The Principles and Practice of Astrology
for home study and college curriculum
by Noel Tyl
in twelve volumes

*A complete, modern restatement of Astrology that is suited
both for study and for reference, for both student and
professional. Its reception and endorsement
by respected authorities and teachers have been sensational.*

I. Horoscope Construction

Here is an unrivaled explanation of the construction of a horoscope.
All time and position corrections are made maximally clear. A totally
self-contained volume, with tables and practice horoscope blanks.
Contents include: calculating the time of birth—step-by-step
guidance, use of materials and examples; measuring the houses—what
they are, how they're placed; the calligraphy—the symbols of
astrology, meaning of the signs, illustrative birthdays of famous
people; placing the planets—measuring planetary movement, test
horoscopes; calculation review—special time problems explained; the
Sun and the signs—the Sun as the key, Sun Sign interpretations, the
elements, polarities, modes; the ruling planets—meaning and function
of planets in the chart with sample horoscopes reviewed; the Age of
Aquarius—what it is and what it means to astrologers.

II. The Houses: Their Signs and Planets

The rationale of house demarcation, the meanings of the signs upon
each house, the planets' significance in every house; derivative house
readings.

III. The Planets: Their Signs and Aspects

A full expansion of the elements and modes in a refreshingly modern style; the significance of every planet within every sign; the reading of aspects and dignities "at a glance"; the suggested meanings of all major aspects and Sun-Moon combinations. An invaluable master reference book for horoscope interpretation.

IV. Aspects and Houses in Analysis

Analytical synthesis technique presented through many examples, showing hemisphere emphasis, retrogradation patterns, the grand trine, the grand square, the T square in complete explanation, the lunar nodal axis, parallels of declination, and the part of fortune; the "law of naturalness." A volume devoted totally to the art of synthesis.

V. Astrology and Personality

Never before presented: an explanation of psychological theories of personality translated into astrological terms and technique! The theories of Kurt Lewin, Carl Jung, Henry Murray, Abraham Maslow, Erich Fromm, Alfred Adler and Sigmund Freud; and astrological glossary of psychological terms and personality traits.

VI. The Expanded Present

An introduction to prediction, an analysis of the time dimension in astrology; application and separation of aspects, "rapport" measurements, secondary progression, primary directions, "factor 7" analysis. Many examples clarify the work of astrology toward understanding change and development in personality, within free-will and fate.

VII. Integrated Transits

A definitive work, modernizing the rationale, analysis and application of transit theory, in accord with the needs and expectations of modern people. Astrology is translated into behavior with many real-life examples for every major transit. The work also includes studies of solar revolution, rectification, eclipse theory, and accidents.

VIII. Analysis and Prediction

A gallery of astrological portraits: the whole-view of astrological analysis; inspection of the past, expansion of the present, the creation of the future. Each step of deduction, analysis, and projection is presented in the sharing of real-life horoscopes: *you* become the astrologer! Radix methods, progressions, and transits are fully interpreted. In addition, there is an introduction to Horary and Electional Astrology.

IX. Special Horoscope Dimensions

Success: vocation, relocation, opportunity, elections. Sex: chart comparison, sex profile, love, homosexuality, abortion, creativity. Illness: health problems, surgery, vitality.

X. Astrological Counsel

Never before presented: a full, detailed inspection of the psychodynamics of the astrologer-client relationship, with examples showing the astrologer's consideration of the horoscope *and* the individual, bringing together the personality and its time structure for fulfillment. Difficulties analyzed, communication techniques explored.

XI. Astrology: Astral, Mundane, Occult

The fixed stars, the individual degrees and decanates; considerations of mundane astrology governing international events; study of death and reincarnation, the areas shared by astrology and occult studies.

XII. Times to Come

A projection of astrology into the future, investigating the potential of astrology. A complete subject index for all twelve volumes.

Teacher's Guide

Not part of the series, but for educators teaching astrology. A complete explanation of all subjects: difficulties, suggested techniques, test examinations for each step of development.